the modern preserver

jams, pickles, cordials, compotes, and more

the modern preserver

jams, pickles, cordials, compotes, and more

kylee newton

The Countryman Press

A division of W. W. Norton & Company

Independent Publishers Since 1923

For my Nan, Lucy May Lovegrove, and my dear friend
Cameron Bain. Both of whom I lost within a week
of each other while writing this book.

Nana May, your strength and love is forever with me.

Cameron, I miss you, thank you for the music.

contents

introduction

I'm a New Zealander based in Hackney, East London, where I have lived and worked for the past 15 years. It is here that I began my preserves company Newton & Pott, a genuinely heartfelt "kitchen table" business, with jars cluttering every surface and pans bubbling on the stove. With the help of my brilliant assistant, Karolina Stein, I make everything by hand and sell my preserves at Broadway Market in Hackney on Saturdays as well as in several delis, pantries, butchers, cafés, and pubs across London.

It was about seven years ago that I first started making chutneys and preserves. I was strapped for cash and wanted to make treats as gifts. Not only did I fall in love with the process of preserving but when I presented people with a jar, they seemed surprisingly touched that it was something I had made myself. This encouraged me to start Newton & Pott so I could share that homemade sentiment with everyone.

I also wanted to waste less. My husband and I use up what we have in the fridge and cupboards. We hate to throw out food. It's a waste of money and resources, a waste of someone's effort to grow, rear, nourish, or harvest that produce. In our consumer society, people unnecessarily throw things out, and expiration dates put the fear into people. But why? We are intelligent enough to judge for ourselves when something has gone bad.

Preserving is an antidote to waste. At Newton & Pott we make the most out of the seasonal harvest and produce past its expiration date, turning it into something that will last. The ethos of preserving is: "saving the season" and "waste not, want not."

Since I started I have learned so much more about this artisan technique: what flavors work best together, the chemistry, the ins and outs of bacteria, and how things ferment. It continues to surprise and inspire me every day. In this book I've set out to surprise and inspire you too so you can introduce preserving to your everyday life without it seeming too daunting.

I've been cooking for as long as I can remember. My sisters and I each cooked the family meal once a week on a rotating basis, and even at age 10 I found this an exciting task: flicking through my mum's 80s cookbook collection, choosing what to make, heading to the market to shop, and preparing a meal for the whole family.

My father was a fisherman; I still love to say, "I'm a fisherman's daughter." We went on several trips out on his boat where we caught many a kahawai, red or blue cod, gurnard, and John Dory, plus the odd octopus or small shark we would have to throw back in the sea. I always remember the feeling of catching my first fish, the adrenaline that rushes through your body, and then the pride when you get home from a catch, being able to feed the whole family something that you had hunted and gathered. Dad would dive and lay crayfish traps while we waited above to see what treasures he emerged with.

Cooking for my family, especially cooking a fish I caught myself, gave me an early feel for the buzz one can get from producing food. So, as a student and when I was traveling, I took jobs in kitchens, cafés, and bars. I couldn't get enough of prepping, cooking, barista-ing, and that's how I supported myself when I first moved to London in 2001.

I made my first-ever preserve when I had been settled in London for a while. I missed home so I turned to the New Zealand cookbook *The Edmonds Cookery Book*. This has been a household name and cookery bible in most New Zealand homes for over 100 years and, via its tomato and apple chutney, I found a way to satisfy my nostalgia. With subsequent batches I started playing around with the flavors and adapting them to my palate: adding spices, taking away dried fruits, lessening the sugar. Now I also dry-salt the tomatoes to drain off excess liquid, and gently toast the cloves so the flavor is not too intense (see page 17).

It's important to be creative with your preserving. Subtract, add, adjust, develop the recipe to your own taste, and constantly learn from what you have made. There is a definite craft to making preserves, and rules to follow, but the most important thing is to play and enjoy. We are lucky this is an era with ready access to new flavors, fruits, and vegetables from around the world. Even within the last few years, unheard-of spices and herbs have become commonplace and easily available. I guess what I'm trying to encourage is creativity. Let travel influence your ideas, spin that flavor wheel and try out new and interesting combinations. This has been my ethos when developing new preserves, and you can adopt it when making your own.

One of the great pleasures of preserving is, literally, giving the fruits of your labor as gifts. Having completed a fine arts degree to working as the personal printer for Turner Prize-winner Wolfgang Tillmans for 10 years before Newton & Pott, I've become a stickler for presentation. I love the way preserving lends itself to creative styling.

My time at Wolfgang's studio in Bethnal Green exposed me to wonderful delights, both visual and culinary. We all took time to sit for 40 minutes at lunch and outdo each other with interesting and exotic flavors from around the world (there was only one English person working there). We served up dishes that ranged from German white asparagus through to ceviche and salads galore. We had oysters brought fresh from Billingsgate Market and there was talk of my miso with shiitake and udon being pipelined to the studio in Berlin when Wolfgang sadly relocated there.

This aesthetic approach to food was a valuable lesson. I realized you can stamp your individual creativity onto the look and taste of your recipes. Things should be both pretty enough to eat and so tasty that you present them at their best.

I live in an urban environment and for me that is an important fact of modern preserving. It needn't be a rural idyll; it is a craft that anyone can get into. You can buy seasonal fruit very cheaply at your local corner store or from your local farmers' or produce market—and although it's best to follow seasons and buy locally, these days supermarkets tend to have what you may need all year round. In Hackney, more and more people are interested in learning about artisan food techniques, and preserving is at the heart of it. People increasingly want to know what goes into their food so preserving the old-fashioned way, without additives, colorings, and preservatives, is enjoying a renaissance.

The great thing about preserving these days is not only is it free from chemicals but also there is a shift toward reducing unnecessary sugar and salt. In the past, making jam felt rather rule-bound; it involved adding a whole lot of refined sugar to ensure a perfect firm set. These days, tastes and techniques have moved on, and when testing my recipes I have put thought into how to cut down the salt and sugar, or use less processed types. For example, in my Caramelized Red Onion Chutney (see page 25) I use unrefined brown sugars. I have also included recipes for continental-style, soft-set jams like Rhubarb and Strawberry Jam (see page 158) which need less sugar to stabilize. And the Pickles, Fermentations, and Vinegars chapter has healthy eating at its heart. It celebrates raw vegetables and good bacteria, which makes preserving a feel-good activity in more ways than one.

there are some rules:

seasonality

Working with the seasons is a crucial part of making preserves. Although today we have access to fruits that are grown all over the world, preserving what is readily available to us is key. Jams taste better using freshly picked fruit, which is not too ripe. At Newton & Pott we only make seasonal jams so our recipes change month by month.

By following the seasons you soon become familiar with the times of year when particular produce is both available and bountiful. Summer through to autumn is, of course, the key harvest time for most fruit and vegetables so it's the busiest period for preserving. By preserving berries, cherries, peaches, apricots, watermelons, cucumbers, greengages, and field rhubarb you can be fully stocked for the colder months ahead. Winter through to spring is a time for damsons, plums, apples and pears, bitter and blood oranges, and forced rhubarb. And some fruits, like damsons, rhubarb, raspberries, cranberries, blueberries, and blackberries freeze really well, so take advantage of this if you want to save your preserving for another day.

bacteria: good and bad

Good: These are the micro-organisms that are created by the breaking down of fruit and vegetable fibers. The naturally occuring yeasts activate the process of fermentation, cultivating probiotic bacteria that are extremely good for your digestive health. These bacteria are great for making fruit vinegars, sauerkraut, and kimchi, but not so great when they start to grow mold.

Bad: When they grow in large numbers, bacteria become a food hazard and it's extremely important to keep them at bay. They thrive when the enzymes in food start to break down, but clean sterile conditions will prevent them developing. They also die off at temperatures over 212°F and become dormant at temperatures below freezing. That is why it's essential to maintain a clean environment when preserving and to practice the sterilizing techniques described (see page 13).

sterilization

Any micro-organism present in your jar or bottle has the potential to become
a health hazard. Practicing cleanliness and proper sterilizing means harmful
bacteria will not multiply.

One way to sterilize your jars, bottles, and lids is by running them through
a hot dishwasher cycle but they need to be hot and completely dry when
you are ready to fill them. I prefer to wash them with hot soapy water
by hand, thoroughly rinse them, then place them in a low-temperature
oven, around 250°F, for at least 20 minutes. I take them out a few minutes
before I want to fill them, while they are still warm and completely dry.
This way I can make sure there is no dishwashing residue left on the glass
that may contaminate the preserve. You can also use a hot water bath or a
commercial sanitizing solution.

Recycle and collect interesting bottles and jars, of different sizes, using
their manufacturers' matching lids with regulation rubber inner seals
(most modern jars have these). If you are using vintage jars or bottles
and the lids are purely metal (without rubber), be aware that old lids will
react to the vinegars and could taint the preserve. So make sure they are
thoroughly cleaned and sterilized before reuse, then add a layer of wax
paper before sealing.

relishes, chutneys, and sauces

When I began making preserves I started with chutneys. It appealed
to me as a way of using up fruit and vegetables, a way of practicing "waste
not, want not" and creating something that I could store in my cupboard
for the months ahead. It seems fitting to start this book off with them.

relishes and chutneys

"What are relishes and chutneys and what is the difference between the
two?" I get asked this a lot at my Newton & Pott stand. Though both are
spiced fruit/vegetable chunky condiments cooked and preserved in sugar
and vinegars, what differentiates them is how they are cooked. Chutney
was introduced to Western cultures from India in the 19th century and is
generally cooked for longer than its fresher, lighter counterpart.
It has a jammier consistency and should have a resting period to allow
the flavors to marry. Relish, which also originated in India and tends to be a
more common term in the US, tends to have a shorter cooking time and is
crunchier. Relishes tend to vary; some need refrigeration and eating within
a week, others can be stored and eaten within six months to a year. But the
two terms can be used interchangeably due to their similarities.

sauces

As for a sauce, this catch-all term can include anything from a fresh, barely
cooked assembly of flavors blended into a light liquid to a slow-cooked
reduction of fruits, vegetables, spices, sugars, and vinegars blended into
a smooth, heavy purée.

key ingredients

Vinegar, sugar, spices, and salt are the important ingredients that make up a chutney.

Vinegar: This is the most important ingredient when preserving chutneys, sauces, and relishes. Its acetic acid content prevents bacteria and molds from growing so make sure you choose ones that have at least 5 percent acetic content. I preserve with all sorts of different vinegars—cider, red wine, white wine—and enjoy pairing them with the flavors of the recipe. Note that rice and rice wine vinegars have less acetic acid so preserves made with these won't last as long, so eat them quite quickly.

Sugar: The type of sugar you use will affect the flavor of your preserve. I vary my sugars, using dark brown, light brown, and granulated, to lend different notes to the recipes. Sometimes I mix it up and use more than one.

Spices: This is where you can really have some fun and make your preserves your own. If you like a particular spice or like extra heat, by all means adjust the spices to taste. Make sure you use freshly ground, crushed or toasted whole spices to release the distinct flavors, unless the recipe specifies pre-ground. Some spices such as chilis or bay leaves may be added for flavor but are not meant to be eaten; put these spices in a clean muslin square and tie this into a bag, using kitchen string, before adding to the pan.

Salt: I usually stir salt through at the end so that it binds all of the flavors together and doesn't concentrate with the evaporation of the long cooking period, though in some recipes the onions are salted while sautéing at the start.

key equipment

- Collection of different-size glass jars and bottles with rubber-sealed lids and caps, sterilized, and completely dry for longer preservation.
- A large stainless steel pan, preferably a wide, heavy-bottomed one with lowish sides. The quicker the pan heats the quicker it will reduce the contents. The wider mass creates more steam bubbles, resulting in a faster reduction, meaning you get the best out of your fruit and vegetables without overcooking. Don't use copper or brass pans: they will react with the acid in the vinegars and taint the flavor of the preserve.
- Wooden spoons: solid with long handles; a longer handle helps when the preserve starts to spit.
- Muslin squares or bags: for holding spices and, if using squares, you'll need kitchen string to tie them up.
- Funnels: one with a wide short spout for chutney, another with a long thin spout for sauces.

- Ladle, glass, or metal jug and a spatula: for pouring and scraping
  out the last bits.
- Blender, food processor, or food mill: for a smoother consistency.
- Tongs: for removing muslin spice bags from the hot preserve.

method tips

- Use up produce that has started to become over-ripe but make sure
  to cut away any brown, bruised, or moldy bits.
- Wash all fruit and vegetables before prepping to remove any dirt
  or unwanted residues.
- Chop the fruit and vegetables into similar-size pieces (chop roughly
  for sauces as these will be blended) and slow-cook the mixture, on
  a moderate heat and at a constant bubbling simmer, allowing the
  liquid to reduce.
- To prepare the spice bag, place spices in a small muslin square and
  secure with kitchen string. If using whole cloves, toast lightly in a pan
  first for a milder clove flavor.
- When you run a wooden spoon across the bottom of the pan and see
  a trail, it's ready; this is known as the "trail test."
- Consistent stirring is important as this releases the bubbles of steam
  allowing the liquid to reduce. Toward the end of the cooking time,
  when the consistency of the preserve is heavier, it becomes harder
  for the steam to escape so it will spit and splatter. Use caution so it
  doesn't burn on the bottom of the pan nor you.
- Remember to remove your muslin spice bag with tongs just before
  you ladle the preserve into your hot jars.
- Always use sterilized jars, bottles, and lids (see page 13 for the
  method). Fill the jar to about $\frac{1}{8}$–$\frac{1}{5}$ inches from the rim with the chutney,
  relish, or sauce and seal with vinegar-proof lids; most modern jars have
  this rubber seal. Clean the rims and sides of the jar before sealing.
- Label the chutney, relish, or sauce with its name and the date it was
  made, then store in a cool, dark place for up to 4 weeks to mature
  before using, unless the recipe states otherwise.
- If you want to double the recipe do so, but add 15–20 percent less
  vinegar and sugar. Otherwise the liquids will take too long to reduce,
  you will overcook the vegetables, and the chutney or sauce could end
  up too sweet.

breaking the rules

Once you become familiar with a few of the general rules, experiment
not only with different fruits, vegetables, and spices but also with how
you eat them. Chutneys, relishes, and sauces go with lots of dishes, not just
cheese, sandwiches, or curries, so be brave and try some of my suggestions!

tomato and apple chutney

This is my recipe adapted from the food bible I grew up with: *The Edmonds Cookery Book*. First published in 1907, it was the essential guide for every young newlywed couple and over the years it has become the bestselling book ever published in New Zealand. It is the first chutney I ever made and continues to be one of my staples.

2 lbs tomatoes (vine preferable)
2 tsp salt
2 lbs unpeeled apples
1 ½ lbs onions
3 cups dark brown sugar
3 ¼ cups distilled malt vinegar
¼ cup raisins

spice bag
½ lemon, quartered
½ lime, quartered
2 Thai chilis, halved
1 cinnamon stick, halved
1 tsp black peppercorns
1 tsp whole cloves (see page 17)

makes
6–7 x 12-ounce jars

how to eat
this is perfect for breakfast with a poached egg on toast, bacon and eggs, a bacon or sausage sandwich. With its clove-spiced undertones, it makes a lovely addition to the Christmas table

The key to this recipe is to drain as much liquid off the tomatoes to begin with and to reduce the chutney until it has thickened to the right consistency.

- Dice the tomatoes, sprinkle with salt, and mix together. Leave for at least 1–2 hours to draw out the liquid.
- Peel, core, and chop the apples into small ⅓-inch pieces; peel and dice the onions.
- Drain off the excess liquid from the tomatoes. Put the tomatoes with the prepared spice bag and all of the other ingredients, except the raisins, in a large, heavy-bottomed pan. Bring to a rapid boil.
- Lower the heat and simmer, stirring continuously for 30–40 minutes, until the chutney begins to thicken.
- Stir in the raisins 10 minutes before the end of the cooking time.
- Use the trail test to check that the chutney is ready, then take off the heat and leave to cool for 5 minutes, stirring to release excess liquid as steam.
- Remove the spice bag, ladle into warm, dry sterilized jars and seal.
- Leave to mature in a cool, dark place for at least 4 weeks.

Keeps for up to 6 months to a year unopened. Once opened, refrigerate and consume within 4 months.

mango salsa chutney

I spent my honeymoon in Mexico, a place I had always wanted to visit. There are mango trees everywhere and they have a huge range of chilis for cooking so I wanted to make a recipe inspired by that trip, something different from the more common Indian-style mango chutney. The result captures the fresh sweetness of mango, then follows up with a punch of heat. Very Mexican.

2 red peppers
1 lb red onions
3 tbsp olive oil
sea salt and freshly ground
    black pepper
2 small garlic cloves
3 Thai chilis
2 limes
2 tbsp fresh ginger
¼ tsp ground cinnamon
½ tsp crushed red pepper
1¼ cup light brown sugar
4 large mangoes
1½ cups cider vinegar

makes
3–4 x 10-ounce jars

season summer

how to eat
this is great in the summer with barbecued or grilled chicken or fish. Eat with smoked or steamed salmon. Or try it with avocado on toast sprinkled with sumac and crushed pistachios

- Preheat the oven to 250°F.
- Halve the red peppers, remove their stalks and seeds, then place them on a baking tray and cook in the oven for at least 1 hour. Once soft and browned, remove from the oven, peel off their skins, then finely slice and dice them.
- Peel and dice the onions. Heat the oil in a heavy-bottomed pan, then add the onions and a little salt and pepper and cook for about 10 minutes, until soft and transparent.
- Meanwhile, peel the garlic, deseed the chilis then finely chop them both.
- Zest the limes, then halve them. Peel and grate the ginger. Add the garlic, chilis, lime zest and halves, ginger, cinnamon, and crushed red pepper to the onions and cook for another 10 minutes.
- Add the sugar to the pan and caramelize for 5 minutes.
- Meanwhile, peel, pit, and cube the mangoes. Add to the pan with the vinegar, and gently bring to boil.
- Simmer, stirring continuously for 20–30 minutes, until the chutney starts to thicken, add the diced red pepper and cook for another 10 minutes.
- Remove from the heat and take out the lime halves. Ladel into warm, dry sterilized jars, then seal.
- You can eat this one the very next day but it will mature nicely if left for at least 4 weeks.

Keeps for up to 6–8 months unopened. Once opened, refrigerate and consume within 4 months.

caramelized fig and ginger relish

Figs are amazing eaten straight from the tree, yes, but they are also a pleasure when found on offer in your corner store in the summer, ripe and ready to be made into relish. Make the most of this fruit when you start to see them appear.

4½ lbs fresh black figs
3 cups dark brown sugar
1½ lbs red onions
1 tbsp olive oil
2 cups white wine vinegar
1 tsp mixed spice
1 tsp ground ginger
1 tsp salt

spice bag
4 tbsp fresh ginger, roughly chopped
1 Thai chili, halved
1½ tsp black peppercorns
1 lemon, quartered

makes
4–5 x 12-ounce jars

how to eat
fabulous with lots of different cheeses

- Trim the ends of the figs and cut each one into 12 pieces. Place in a bowl, stir in 1½ cups of the sugar and leave to macerate for 1 hour.
- Peel and slice the onions finely on a mandoline and put in a large jam pan or heavy-bottomed pan with the oil. Sweat for 10 minutes, then add the remaining sugar.
- Caramelize the sugar and the onions for another 10 minutes, then add the figs and their sugary syrup. Cook for an additional 10 minutes on a moderate heat.
- Add all the remaining ingredients, including the prepared spice bag, to the pan. Raise the heat and bring to a boil.
- Lower the heat to a simmer, then stir continuously for 30–40 minutes, until the chutney begins to thicken. Use the trail test to check when it is ready, then remove from the heat, take out the spice bag, ladle into warm, dry sterilized jars and seal.
- Can be eaten immediately but best left to mature for at least 4 weeks.

Keeps for up to 6 months to a year unopened. Once opened, refrigerate and consume within 4 months.

hot spiced apple chutney

When apple season comes around, use an extra bushel to make this spicy and savory chutney. Underripe plums would also work well.

4 lbs apples
½ lb onions
2 garlic cloves
4 Thai chilis
3 tbsp fresh ginger
1 tsp yellow mustard seeds
½ tsp coriander seeds
¼ tsp cumin seeds
3 limes, zest only
3 cups white wine vinegar
3 cups light brown sugar
2 tsp salt

spice bag
½ tsp allspice berries (or ¼
    tsp ground)
1 small cinnamon stick
1 tsp black peppercorns
1 star anise
2 green cardamom pods

makes
4–5 x 12-ounce jars

season late summer/ early fall

how to eat
best eaten with cheese and crackers accompanied with charcuterie and pickles

- Peel, core, and chop the apples into small ⅓-inch pieces. Peel and dice the onions and finely chop the peeled garlic and the chilis into small pieces. Peel and finely grate the ginger then gently crush/mash the mustard, coriander, and cumin seeds together using a mortar and pestle.
- Place all of the ingredients, except the salt, with the prepared spice bag into a large, heavy-bottomed pan and bring to a boil.
- Reduce on a steady simmer, stirring intermittently, for up to 1½ hours. Stir frequently towards the end as bubbles will form on the bottom. Use caution, as the chutney will spit.
- Once the chutney has thickened, and the trail test shows that it is ready, take off the heat and stir in the salt.
- Remove the spice bag and then ladle into warm, dry sterilized jars and seal.
- Mature in a cool, dark cupboard for at least 4 weeks.

Keeps for up to 6 months to a year unopened. Once opened, keep refrigerated and eat within 4 months.

caramelized red onion chutney

This one is a favorite. I like to think mine is a little different with its undertones of balsamic vinegar and the slight kick of chili to finish it off. It is less sweet than others I've tried and perhaps that is why this recipe has been known to convert non-chutney enthusiasts.

4 lbs red onions
1 tbsp olive oil
2 cups dark brown sugar
2 tsp red chili flakes
1½ lbs apples
1¾ cups balsamic vinegar
½ cup red wine vinegar
2 tsp salt

spice bag
2 bay leaves
1 lime, quartered
1 tsp black peppercorns

makes
5–6 x 12-ounce jars

how to eat
this one's lovely with goat cheese and roasted pepper toasted sandwiches, or make goat cheese mini-tarts and put a dollop on top. Especially delicious on a burger

- Peel and slice the onions into very thin slices (with a mandoline if you have one).
- Sweat the onions in the oil on a low heat in a large, heavy-bottomed pan until soft and transparent; this takes about 10–15 minutes. Be careful not to burn them as this makes them bitter.
- Add the sugar and chili flakes and caramelize the softened onions for another 15 minutes.
- Peel, core, and dice the apples and prepare your spice bag. Add both to the onions with the vinegars.
- Bring to boil, then leave to simmer, stirring intermittently so it doesn't stick and burn on the bottom, for around 30–40 minutes or until the moisture has dried out and the trail test lets you know it is ready.
- At the end of the cooking time, add the salt and stir in thoroughly.
- Remove the spice bag and then ladle into warm, dry sterilized jars. It's a very stringy chutney so if it needs encouragement to get into the jars, push the mixture down with a spoon to get rid of as many of the air bubbles as possible.
- Store in a cool, dark place for at least 4 weeks before eating.

Keeps for up to 6 months to a year unopened. Once opened, keep refrigerated and eat within 4 months.

dr. ben's chili jam

Dr. Ben's family has an annual chutney competition, trophy and all. I entered one year (as an honorary family member, cousin-in-law or something) and came sixth. They told me that was a good result as there's a large family involvement. This is the recipe which won that year. I had to have it, and now you have it too.

2 tbsp olive oil
1 lb ripe plum or vine tomatoes
3 large garlic cloves
sea salt and freshly ground
   black pepper
3 tbsp fresh ginger
6 Thai chilis
1 tbsp fish sauce
½ cup red wine vinegar
1 cup light muscovado sugar
½ tsp Chinese five-spice powder

makes
1–2 x 10-ounce jars

how to eat
hot, spicy and improves with age so if you can wait a month or even two, do! Try it with cheese or spread it thinly on the layers of a baked eggplant, tomato, mozzarella, and basil panini smothered in melted cheese

The key to this chutney/jam is good-quality ripe tomatoes and roasting them first.

- Preheat the oven to 425°F.
- Measure the olive oil into a roasting pan and heat in the hot oven until smoking.
- Halve the tomatoes and toss them and the unpeeled garlic cloves in the hot oil. Season generously, then roast for 20–25 minutes until caramelized.
- Remove the tomatoes and garlic from the oven and remove the skins from the garlic cloves.
- Peel and roughly chop the ginger, deseed and chop the chilis, then blend with the tomatoes, garlic and fish sauce in a blender or food processor until you have a rough paste.
- In a heavy-bottomed pan, mix the paste with the vinegar, sugar, and five-spice and bring to a boil.
- Simmer and reduce for about 30–40 minutes, stirring intermittently, then use the trail test to check when it is ready.
- Ladle into warm, dry sterilized jars and seal.
- Store in a cool, dark cupboard for at least 4 weeks to mature.

Keeps for up to 6 months to a year unopened. Once opened, keep refrigerated and eat within 4 months.

feijoa chutney

If you have friends from New Zealand you are bound to have heard them talking about feijoas at some stage. This small guava-like fruit is sweet and fragrant with a slight medicinal aroma. Gritty in texture, it is sometimes described as tasting like a cross between pineapple, apple and mint. It is native to South America but can be found growing in most New Zealand home gardens. If you can't find feijoa near you, just substitute the same amount of guava.

1½ lbs feijoas
1 lb apples
1 lb onions
2½ cups light brown sugar
2½ cups cider vinegar
⅛ tsp ground mace
¼ tsp cayenne pepper
1½ tsp garam masala
1 tsp salt

spice bag
½ lemon, quartered
1 tbsp fresh ginger, sliced
½ tsp black peppercorns

makes
5–6 x 12-ounce jars

season feijoas are imported all year round

how to eat
great with creamy cheeses such as Brie and Camembert or with softer blues like Roquefort

- Peel and dice the feijoas into ⅓-inch pieces. Peel, core, and dice the apples to a similar size. Peel and finely chop the onions.
- Prepare your spice bag and place it with all the other ingredients, except the salt, in a heavy-bottomed, wide-rimmed pan, and bring to a rapid boil.
- Lower the heat slightly and simmer, stirring constantly, making sure it doesn't stick to the bottom and burn.
- Reduce and thicken for about 20–30 minutes stirring through the salt in the last 10 minutes, using the trail test to check when it is ready.
- Remove from the heat, discard the spice bag then ladle into warm, dry sterilized jars and seal.
- Mature in a cool, dark cupboard for at least 4 weeks.

Keeps for up to 6 months to a year unopened. Once opened, refrigerate and eat within 4 months.

red currant and red onion relish

Red currants remind me of jewels; they are just as pretty and precious. My grandmother in-law grows them in a caged section of her large garden in Southampton. She's 93 now and not as able to venture out to pick them herself, so I love to go there and steal them to make my preserves—it makes me feel like a jewel thief.

3 lbs red currants
3 lbs red onions
2 tbsp rapeseed oil
4–6 garlic cloves
3 tbsp fresh ginger
4 Thai chilis
3 cups red wine vinegar
2 tsp ground allspice
1 tsp salt
4¾ cups dark brown sugar

makes
5–6 x 12-ounce jars

season summer

how to eat
delicious served with cold meats and cheese, particularly goat cheese and other soft crumbly cheeses

- Remove the currants gently from their stalks and rinse carefully. Peel and dice the onions.
- Heat the oil in a large, heavy-bottomed pan on a low heat, add the onions, and cook them until soft and transparent.
- Meanwhile, peel and finely chop the garlic, peel and finely grate the ginger, and deseed and chop the chilis (leave in the seeds if you want a hotter relish). Add the garlic, ginger, and chilis to the onions and fry for another 3–5 minutes, stirring regularly.
- Add the red wine vinegar, ground allspice, salt, and sugar and bring to boil. Steadily boil for at least 15 minutes, stirring constantly to prevent the relish sticking to the bottom of the pan.
- Add the red currants and continue to boil and stir for another 30–40 minutes, until you have a sticky consistency. Use the trail test to check when it's ready.
- Remove from the heat, ladle into warm, dry sterilized jars and seal.
- Mature in a cool, dark cupboard for at least 2–4 weeks.

Keeps for up to 6 months to a year unopened. Once opened, refrigerate and eat within 4 months.

pineapple and star anise relish

Don't be too scared of this 70s combo. It reminds me of creeping downstairs at one of my parents' parties when I was little and peeking at them drunkenly dancing around the sofa. And also of sneaking that delicious pineapple-and-cheese treat arranged just-so on toothpicks. It's very *Abigail's Party* and it tastes just as brashly fantastic.

2 lbs fresh pineapple
1¾ cups white wine vinegar
1½ cups light brown sugar
1 tbsp fresh ginger
1 lime, zest and juice
1 tsp freshly ground black pepper
2 tsp chili flakes
2 star anise
½ cinnamon stick
1 lemongrass stalk, halved
½ lb onions

makes
4 x 12-ounce jars

how to eat
with cheese but also great with Thai food such as fish cakes

- Prepare the pineapple: Trim the ends, then slice off the skin. Cut into ¾-inch discs, then into bite-size cubes.
- Mix the vinegar and sugar in a large, heavy-bottomed pan, place on a moderate heat and cook until the sugar has dissolved and the liquid has reduced by a third.
- While the liquid is cooking, peel and slice the ginger.
- Add the ginger, lime zest and juice, pepper, chili flakes, star anise, cinnamon, and lemongrass to the pan and cook for 5–10 minutes.
- Meanwhile, peel and dice the onions.
- Once the mixture thickens, add the pineapple and onions, bring to a boil and cook, stirring intermittently, for another 20–30 minutes, letting the mixture thicken more.
- Remove from the heat, fish out the ginger, star anise, cinnamon stick, and lemongrass, then ladle into warm, dry sterilized jars and seal.
- Can be eaten immediately but best left to mature in the fridge for 2–4 weeks before opening.

Keeps for up to 6 months to a year unopened. Once opened, keep refrigerated and consume within 4 months.

roasted red pepper and tomato relish

This recipe is like a Mediterranean ratatouille but as a relish. It shares ratatouille's sweet, deep, summer-vegetable flavors but preserves them for enjoying in the depths of the cold, winter months.

2 lbs tomatoes (preferably vine)
olive oil
sea salt and freshly ground
 black pepper
2 lbs red peppers
1 lb zucchinis
1¾ lbs red onions
3 garlic cloves
1 tsp coriander seeds
4 cups dark brown sugar
3¼ cups distilled malt vinegar
2 tsp smoked paprika
¼ tsp ground mace

spice bag
½ lemon, quartered
4 Thai chilis, halved
2 tsp black peppercorns
2 bay leaves

makes
6–7 x 12-ounce jars

how to eat
great in any sandwich or with
a coconut-based curry and rice

All the vegetables need to be roasted but for different times and at different temperatures, so it's best to roast them first, then make the relish the next day.

- Preheat the oven to 285°F.
- Halve the tomatoes, place on a baking tray, cut side up, sprinkle with olive oil and salt and pepper and slowly roast for 1–1½ hours.
- Meanwhile, halve and deseed the red peppers, cut the zucchinis on the diagonal to make long, thin slices, peel the onions and cut each one into 8 wedges. When the tomatoes are done, remove them from the oven and raise the temperature to 350°F.
- Place the peppers, cut side down, zucchinis, onions, and unpeeled garlic cloves on a baking tray, sprinkle with olive oil, season with salt and pepper, then bake for 50 minutes.
- The next day, crush the coriander seeds using a mortar and pestle, remove the skins from the garlic, and roughly chop. Put the roasted vegetables, garlic, coriander seeds, prepared spice bag, and all the other ingredients in a large, heavy-bottomed pan and bring to a boil. Lower the heat and reduce, stirring frequently for 30–40 minutes or until you have reached the right consistency using the trail test.
- Remove the spice bag. Ladle into warm, dry sterilized jars and seal.
- Can be eaten immediately but, if possible, let it mature in a cool, dark place for at least 4 weeks.

Keeps for up to 6 months to a year unopened. Once opened, refrigerate and eat within 4 months.

sticky chili peach jam

Peaches are a delightful fruit. They are very sweet, just like this jam. And to sweeten
it more, I've added dates, raisins, and mixed citris peel, which makes it a good one for
Christmas or to give as a gift to those who like it a bit on the sweet side.

3 lbs peaches
1 ½ large garlic cloves
3 ½ cups distilled malt vinegar
½ lb dates
4 ½ cups dark brown sugar
¾ cups mixed citris peel
¾ cups raisins
2 tsp salt
1 tsp cayenne pepper
2 tsp chili flakes

spice bag
1 lime, quartered
1 tsp black peppercorns
1 star anise

makes
5–6 x 12-ounce jars

season summer to early autumn

how to eat
best with cheese and crackers and/or
with charcuterie and pickles

- Pit the peaches and chop into cubes. Peel and
  finely chop the garlic.
- Put the peaches with the vinegar and the
  chopped garlic into a heavy-bottomed pan,
  and cook until soft and starting to break down.
- Meanwhile, pit and dice the dates, prepare the
  spice bag, then add both to the peaches with
  all the remaining ingredients.
- Bring to boil, then simmer for 30–40 minutes,
  stirring often so it doesn't stick to the bottom of
  the pan and burn.
- Once reduced to a sticky consistency and the
  trail test shows it's ready, remove from the heat
  and take out the spice bag. Ladle into warm,
  dry sterilized jars and seal.
- Mature in a cool, dark cupboard for at least
  4 weeks.

Keeps for up to 6 months to a year unopened.
Once opened, keep refrigerated and eat within
4 months.

tamarillo chutney

Tamarillos are indigenous to South America but somehow made their way to the shores of New Zealand. I have been eating them since I was a child. My mother would simply peel and slice them, sprinkle them with sugar, and leave them in the fridge overnight to create a sticky, syrupy topping for our morning shredded wheats (see Tamarillos in Syrup, page 204). They are a magic bittersweet fruit, and, if I was forced to choose, this would be my very favorite chutney.

10–12 tamarillos
1¾ lbs onions
¾ lb apples
1¾ cups white wine vinegar
3½ cups dark brown sugar
2 tsp salt
⅓ cups raisins

spice bag
1 tbsp fresh ginger, sliced
1½ tsp black peppercorns
½ lime, quartered
2 Thai chilis, quartered
1 cinnamon stick, halved

makes
6–7 x 12-ounce jars

season imported all year round

how to eat
this is best eaten with a poached egg on sourdough toast, or with roast duck or on a roast beef sandwich

The key to this recipe is reduction. Tamarillos release a lot of liquid so it's best to keep reducing and thickening it. But it will still be wetter than other chutney recipes.

- Cut a cross in the base of each of the tamarillos and blanch in boiling water for 1–2 minutes; this allows the skin to peel off with ease. Peel, then dice.
- Peel and dice the onions and core, peel and dice the apples.
- Prepare the spice bag and put with the tamarillos, onions, and apples into a heavy-bottomed pan with the vinegar and sugar, then bring to a boil.
- Simmer for around 40 minutes, stirring often until it thickens. Stir constantly towards the end so it doesn't stick and burn on the bottom of the pan.
- Add the salt and raisins and continue to simmer for another 10–15 minutes or until using the trail test shows that it is ready.
- Remove the spice bag and rest the chutney off the heat for at least 5 minutes, stirring to allow more of the liquid in the mixture to evaporate.
- Ladle into warm, dry sterilized jars and seal.
- Store in a cool, dark cupboard for at least 4 weeks to mature.

Keeps for up to 6 months to a year unopened. Once opened, keep refrigerated and eat within 4 months.

spiced zucchini relish

This fruit—yes, botanically it's considered one—makes a delicious relish when combined with a hot and spicy twist of chili and mustard. If you have the zucchini flowers as well, stuff them with ricotta, mint, and pine nuts, batter, and deep-fry them, then serve with the relish on the side.

¾ lb onions
3 lbs zucchini (courgettes)
½ cup light brown sugar
1 tbsp white wine vinegar
1½ tsp ajwan or caraway seeds
1½ tsp brown mustard seeds
1 tsp chili flakes
½ lemon, zest only
1½ tsp sea salt

makes
4–5 x 12-ounce jars

season summer to early autumn

how to eat
great with fritters, from corn to tofu

- Peel and finely chop the onions, dice the zucchini and put both with all the other ingredients, except the salt, into a large, heavy-bottomed pan and bring to a boil.
- Reduce to a simmer on a moderate heat and cook, stirring intermittently, for about 30–40 minutes, so that most of the liquid evaporates.
- Once reduced, use the trail test to check that it is ready then add the salt and mix through.
- Remove from the heat, ladle into warm, dry sterilized jars and seal.
- Can be eaten immediately but best left to mature in the fridge for 2–4 weeks before opening.

Keeps for up to 6 months to a year unopened. Once opened, keep refrigerated and consume within 3–4 weeks.

blackberry relish

You can use blackberries, loganberries, or boysenberries for this recipe, whatever is in season and readily available. My husband hadn't heard of boysenberries and, because of my accent, he always thought I was saying poison berries. He thought this a little odd but kept quiet until, on a trip to New Zealand, he saw boysenberry written on an ice cream container in a supermarket and finally made the connection.

½ lb red onions
1 tbsp fresh ginger
1 orange, zest only
1¾ lbs blackberries/loganberries/
    boysenberries
¾ cup water
1 tsp chili flakes
½ tsp ground cinnamon
sea salt and freshly ground
    black pepper
1¼ cups superfine granulated sugar
1¼ cups red wine vinegar

makes
2–3 x 10-ounce jars

season late summer to early autumn

how to eat
delicious with lamb

- Peel and dice the onions, peel and finely grate the ginger, and put both into a large, heavy-bottomed saucepan. Add the orange zest, berries, water, chili flakes and cinnamon and bring to boil. Cook gently until the berries start to burst.
- Season with salt and pepper, add the sugar and vinegar, and simmer, stirring constantly for an additional 20–30 minutes, until the liquid reduces to a sticky consistency.
- Use the trail test to check when it is ready then ladle into warm, dry sterilized jars and seal.
- Can be eaten immediately but best left for 2–4 weeks to mature.

Keeps for up to 6 months to a year unopened. Once opened, refrigerate and eat within 4 months.

beet and orange chutney

The combination of beets and orange is deliciously colorful and flavorful, made to excite both your eyes and your palate. Beets are naturally quite sweet so, depending on your taste, you can increase or reduce the amount of sugar in this recipe. The whole coriander and mustard seeds add great pops of spice to titillate your palate.

3 lbs beets, uncooked
1 lb red onions
2 lbs apples
2½ tsp yellow mustard seeds
1 tsp coriander seeds
2 tsp pumpkin pie spice mix
2½ cups red wine vinegar
2 cups raw sugar
2–3 oranges, zest and juice

makes
5–6 x 12-ounce jars

season late summer to autumn

how to eat
perfect after dinner with cheese, particularly goat cheese, blue cheese, and mature English cheddar. Add it to your veggie or beef burger instead of ketchup or relish

- Peel and dice the beets into ⅓-inch cubes, peel and chop the onions and peel, core, and dice the apples. Put into a large, heavy-bottomed pan.
- With a mortar and pestle, lightly bash the mustard and coriander seeds. Add these to the pan along with the pumpkin pie spice, vinegar, sugar, orange zest, and juice.
- Bring to boil, then leave simmering on a moderate heat for 40–60 minutes, stirring intermittently, so it doesn't stick and burn on the bottom.
- After 40 minutes check the consistency. The ingredients should have reduced down and be thick and syrupy. Use the trail test to test that it is ready.
- Once thickened, turn off the heat and ladle into warm, dry sterilized jars and seal. Store in a cool, dark cupboard for at least 4 weeks before opening.

Keeps for up to 6 months to a year unopened. Once opened, keep refrigerated and eat within 4 months.

tomato kasundi

This is the best tomato chutney. It comes from India and is full of lots of wonderful Indian spices, which give it a fiery heat. Though very simple to make it is super versatile and matches beautifully with many dishes.

3 lbs tomatoes
2½ tsp salt
9 garlic cloves
¾ cups fresh ginger
1 tsp coriander seeds
10 Thai chilis
½ lb onions
¾ lb apples
1½ cups cider vinegar
2½ tbsp black mustard seeds
3 tbsp olive oil
1 tbsp cumin seeds
1 tbsp ground turmeric
2½ tbsp nigella seeds
½ tsp whole cloves
1 tsp chili powder
1 cup dark brown sugar

makes
5–6 x 12-ounce jars

how to eat
lovely with samosas, curries or rice dishes. Or straight out of the jar on naan bread

Measure and prep all the ingredients first, to make it easier and faster to cook.

- Roughly chop the tomatoes, stir in the salt and leave to steep for about an hour. Meanwhile, prep all the other ingredients: peel and chop the garlic and ginger, crush the coriander seeds, finely chop the chilis, peel and finely dice the onions and peel, core and chop the apples into ⅓-inch cubes.
- Warm the vinegar on a low heat in a small saucepan, add the mustard seeds, then remove from the heat and leave to infuse for 15 minutes.
- Put the garlic and ginger into a blender and pulse a few times. Add the vinegar and mustard seed infusion and blend into a smooth paste.
- Heat the oil in a large, heavy-bottomed saucepan on a high heat for 1 minute. Take off the heat for a moment, then add the crushed coriander seeds, cumin seeds, turmeric, nigella seeds, cloves, and chili powder.
- Fry on a moderate heat for 20 seconds then add the mustard-vinegar paste and the chilis and onions. Fry for another 5–10 minutes.
- Drain the excess liquid from the tomatoes and add to the pan with the apples and sugar.
- Reduce the heat and simmer gently for an hour, stirring occasionally.
- Ladle into warm, dry sterilized jars and seal.
- Can be eaten immediately but also great if left to mature in a cool, dark place for 4 weeks if you can.

Keeps for up to a year unopened. Once opened, refrigerate and eat within 4 months.

green bean and coconut relish

Chilis, coconut, and green beans combine here to make a pickled relish with bite. This recipe is light and spicy and can be served as a side dish like a preserved salad, or added to a sandwich for texture and crunch.

2 lbs French green beans
³/₄ cups water
1½ tsp granulated sugar
1 tsp sea salt
1 lb onions
3 Thai chilis
2 garlic cloves
6¼ cups cider vinegar
1½ cups light brown sugar
3 tbsp cornflour
1½ tsp ground turmeric
1½ tsp mustard powder
1 tsp yellow mustard seeds
1 cup coconut flakes

makes
6–7 x 12-ounce jars

how to eat
straight from the jar or serve
as a side dish

- Trim and slice the beans into ³/₄-inch pieces.
- Boil the water in a pan with the granulated sugar and salt, add the trimmed and sliced beans and boil for about 3–4 minutes, so that they are still crunchy, then remove from the heat, drain, and immediately dunk the beans in iced water for 2 minutes so that they stop cooking. Drain.
- Peel and dice the onions, finely chop the chilis and peel and finely chop the garlic. Gently cook the onions with 3 cups of the vinegar in a large, heavy-bottomed pan for 5 minutes then add the beans, chilis, garlic, brown sugar, and remaining vinegar. Cook for another 5 minutes, stirring all the time.
- In a bowl, mix together the cornflour, turmeric, mustard powder, and mustard seeds with about 1 teaspoon of water to make a thick wet paste, then add this to the bean pan and stir through.
- Add the coconut flakes and simmer on a moderate heat for another 10–15 minutes until the mixture thickens, stirring intermittently so it doesn't catch on the bottom of the pan. Use the trail test to check that it is ready.
- Remove from the heat, ladle into warm, dry sterilized jars, and seal.
- Can be eaten immediately but best left to mature in the fridge for 2–4 weeks before opening.

Keeps in the fridge for up to 6 months unopened. Once opened, refrigerate and consume within 3–4 weeks.

eggplant, juniper, and tomato chutney

Although eggplants don't make the prettiest chutney, it is one of the most delicate and flavorsome ingredients. Don't be put off by the color, and enjoy.

1 ½ lbs eggplants (3–4 large)
1 tbsp olive oil
1 ½ tsp juniper berries
¾ lb tomatoes
½ lb apples
3 red onions
2 garlic cloves
2 Thai chilis
¾ cup dark brown sugar
1 ¼ cup red wine vinegar
¾ tsp cumin seeds
¾ tsp brown mustard seeds
1 ½ tsp sea salt

makes
4–5 x 12-ounce jars

how to eat
with a greasy breakfast after a hard night out

- Preheat the oven to 350°F.
- Cut the eggplants lengthwise, score the flesh diagonally in both directions, place on a baking tray, sprinkle with the oil and juniper berries and bake for 40 minutes.
- Meanwhile, chop the tomatoes into $\frac{1}{3}$-inch cubes, peel, core, and dice the apples, peel and chop the onions, peel and finely chop the garlic and finely chop the chilis.
- Remove the eggplants from the oven and leave to cool. Then chop, skin-on, into $\frac{1}{3}$-inch cubes and place in a large, heavy-bottomed pan with the juniper berries and all the other ingredients, except the salt, and bring to boil.
- Reduce to a moderate heat and simmer, stirring intermittently, for 20–30 minutes until most of the liquid has evaporated. It will thicken quickly and become quite mushy in consistency.
- Use the trail test to check when it is ready, then stir through the salt.
- Remove from the heat, ladle into warm, dry sterilized jars and seal.
- Can be eaten immediately but is best left to mature for at least 4 weeks.

Keeps for up to 6 months to a year unopened. Once opened, refrigerate and consume within 4 months.

plum and almond chutney

If you love a sharp vinegary bite to your chutney, try this. The addition of the flaked nuts gives this preserve texture, and its nuttiness is wonderful with gorgonzola. It's the perfect chutney for Christmas—make it three months before so that the flavors marry in time.

5 lbs plums
3 large onions
½ cup fresh ginger
4 lemons, zest and juice (you
   need 1 cup juice)
1¼ cup light brown sugar
1¾ cups red wine vinegar
1½ tsp chilli flakes
½ cup slivered almonds

spice bag
2 small cinnamon sticks
2 star anise

makes
5–6 x 12-ounce jars

season summer to early autumn

how to eat
best eaten with cheese and a glass
of tawny port

Use firmer plums for this recipe.

- Pit the plums and roughly chop them. Peel and dice the onions and peel and grate the ginger.
- Prepare your spice bag and put it in a heavy-bottomed pan with all of the ingredients except the almonds.
- Bring to boil, then simmer for 40–60 minutes, stirring, until the plums are tender. This chutney will spit a lot when reducing so be careful when stirring.
- Add the almonds and cook for another 5 minutes. This chutney thickens differently from other fruit chutneys and remains slightly liquid.
- Remove from the heat, take out the spice bag, and leave to cool for 5 minutes; it will thicken as it cools.
- Ladle into warm, dry sterilized jars and seal.
- Mature in a cool, dark cupboard for 1–3 months before opening.

Keeps for up to 6 months to a year unopened. Once opened, keep refrigerated and eat within 4 months.

carrot and citrus relish

If you want to make chutney in winter and there's not much seasonal produce on hand, this is the chutney to turn to. It tastes delicious with spicy food like curries or onion bhajis.

¾ lb onions
1¾ lbs carrots
1 tbsp fresh ginger
1 tbsp olive oil
1 orange, zest and juice
1 lime, zest and juice
1 lemon, zest and juice
1¾ cups cider vinegar
¾ cup water
1½ cups light brown sugar
3 sprigs fresh lemon thyme
sea salt and freshly ground
   black pepper

makes
4–5 x 8-ounce jars

how to eat
I like to eat this with Indian-inspired dishes

- Peel and finely dice the onions, then peel and grate the carrots and ginger.
- Warm the oil in a large, heavy-bottomed pan and sweat the onions for 5–10 minutes. Add the rest of the ingredients and bring to boil on a high heat for 5 minutes.
- Reduce the heat and simmer gently for up to an hour, stirring intermittently, until the mixture becomes thick and using the trail test shows that it is ready.
- Ladle into warm, dry sterilized jars and seal.
- Can be eaten immediately but best left to mature in the fridge for 2–4 weeks before opening.

Keeps in the fridge for up to 6 months unopened. Once opened, refrigerate and eat within 3–4 weeks.

cranberry, port, and orange sauce

Once you've had this cranberry sauce for your Christmas or Thanksgiving dinner, you'll never go back to a store-bought one. This is fresh, tart, and boozy with a lovely orange-scented aroma. It is also very easy.

1 lb cranberries
1 cup superfine granulated sugar
½ cup water
1 orange, zest and juice (you need
   ½ cup juice)
¾ tsp ground cinnamon
½ cup port, tawny or ruby

makes
3 x 10-ounce jars

season generally autumn
to Christmas

how to eat
serve warm or at room temperature
with your Christmas turkey or
chicken, with cheese, or in a cold
turkey, ham, or Brie sandwich

If you want a larger quantity of cranberry sauce, simply double the ingredients and cook for another 5–10 minutes.

- Put the cranberries in a large, heavy-bottomed pan with the superfine granulated sugar, water, orange zest, orange juice, and cinnamon and bring to boil.
- Wait and listen for the cranberries to pop, about 5–10 minutes. When they have started to open and soften, lightly mash them to let out all the pectin so that the sauce thickens.
- Stir in the port and cook on a moderate heat for 5 minutes or until the sauce thickens again.
- Remove from the heat, ladle into warm, dry sterilized jars and seal.

Best eaten immediately. Once opened, keep in the fridge and eat within 1–2 weeks.

homemade ketchup

Homemade ketchup is the best thing. Store-bought ketchup is basically sugar and salt, which explains why most children (and adults) are addicted. This recipe puts something a lot healthier on your fries: some of its sweetness comes from the apples, so it has a lower sugar content than its commercial counterpart, and its salt content is minimal as well.

4 lbs tomatoes (preferably vine)
1 tbsp salt
1 lb apples
1 lb onions
1 cup raw granulated sugar
1¼ cups distilled malt vinegar
¼ tsp cayenne pepper
1 tsp ground allspice

spice bag
1 tsp black peppercorns
1 tsp whole cloves, lightly toasted
    (see page 17)
1 bay leaf
¼ tsp chilli flakes

makes
4–5 x 17-ounce bottles

how to eat
with homemade fish and chips and burgers or anything else you like eating with ketchup

The key to this recipe is to drain off as much of the excess liquid from the tomatoes as possible. This makes the sauce nice and thick.

- Roughly chop the tomatoes, place in a large bowl and gently stir through the salt. Leave to steep for at least 3 hours. If you don't want tomato skins in your ketchup, blanch the tomatoes to remove the skins before chopping and salting.
- Meanwhile, peel, core and dice the apples and peel and roughly chop the onions.
- Drain off the excess salted liquid from the tomatoes and prepare the spice bag. Put the tomatoes and spice bag, along with all the other ingredients, in a large, heavy-bottomed pan and bring to boil.
- Simmer and stir steadily for 1 hour until the mixture has thickened and reduced by around a third.
- Remove the spice bag and leave to cool then use a food processor or a food mill to blend the mixture to a smooth sauce-like consistency.
- Return the sauce to the pan and bring to boil once again, simmering and stirring for another 20 minutes, skimming off any scum on the surface as it reduces.
- Remove from the heat once it is as thick as you want it.
- Using a funnel, ladle or pour the ketchup into warm, dry sterilized bottles.
- Gently tap the bottom of the bottles on a hard surface to remove any air bubbles, then seal.
- Can be eaten immediately but best left to mature for 2–4 weeks before opening.

Keeps for up to 6 months to a year unopened. Once opened, refrigerate and eat within 4 months.

roasted red pepper ketchup

Good things come to those who wait. This recipe takes a bit of prep and cooking time but it is worth it. It tastes incredible with French fries. Once you try it you may never eat tomato ketchup again.

4½ lbs red peppers
1⅓ lbs apples
1⅓ lbs onions
3 Thai chilis
3 cups distilled malt vinegar
4 cups water
1 cup raw granulated sugar
1 tbsp salt

spice bag
1 lime, quartered
2 tsp black peppercorns
5 sprigs fresh thyme
2 bay leaves

makes
3–4 x 17-ounce bottles

how to eat
use instead of tomato ketchup on homemade chips, fried eggs, or battered fish

- Preheat the oven to 350°F. Trim and deseed the red peppers, then place them, cut side down, on a baking tray. Roast for 50 minutes until the skins have charred.
- Meanwhile, peel, core, and dice the apples, peel and chop the onions, deseed and chop the chilis and prepare the spice bag. When the peppers are done, remove from the oven, leave to cool, then peel and discard skins and roughly chop the flesh.
- Place the pepper flesh in a large, heavy-bottomed pan with the apples, onions, chilis, vinegar, water, and the spice bag and bring to a rapid boil.
- Lower to a moderate heat and cook, stirring steadily for 30–40 minutes, until the vegetables have softened.
- Take off the heat, remove the spice bag, and leave to cool.
- Once cool, purée in a blender, then press through a fine-mesh sieve discarding any excess pulp.
- Return the sieved purée to a clean pan, add the sugar and salt, and simmer gently for another 45–60 minutes, stirring frequently until it has reduced and thickened to a sauce-like consistency. Be careful when stirring as the sauce will spit.
- Once ready, remove from the heat and pour the ketchup through a funnel into warm, dry sterilized bottles.
- Gently tap the bottom of the bottles on a hard surface to remove any air bubbles, then seal.
- Can be eaten immediately but best left to mature for 2–4 weeks before opening.

Keeps for up to 6 months to a year unopened. Once opened, refrigerate and eat within 4 months.

homemade chinese plum sauce

In China, people have been cooking with plums for over 3,000 years and they are celebrated as a symbol of endurance and strength because they survive the long cold winters. In other countries, plums start to appear early in the summer and they last until early autumn. If you live in a city, like I do, where there are plum trees, you will have been lucky enough to experience their beautiful blossom in the spring.

4½ lbs plums
1 lb red onions
4–6 garlic cloves
2¼ cups granulated sugar
2 cups cider vinegar
⅓ cup good-quality soy sauce
1 tbsp ground ginger
1 tbsp English mustard powder
1 tsp ground cinnamon
1 tsp cayenne pepper
½ tsp ground cloves

makes
3–4 x 17-ounce bottles

season early summer to early autumn

how to eat
use as a dip with summer rolls,
duck pancakes, or pork buns

- Pit and chop the plums, peel and dice the onions and peel and grate the garlic. Purée them together in a food processor or blender, in batches, until smooth and put in a large, heavy-bottomed pan.
- Add all of the other ingredients and bring to a boil, stirring regularly to prevent the sauce sticking to the bottom of the pan and burning.
- Simmer and stir steadily for 60–70 minutes until the sauce has thickened and reduced by about a third, keeping in mind it will thicken more once it cools. If it needs to be thicker, mix a little cornflour with water and add a little at a time until it is the right consistency.
- Using a funnel or ladle, pour the sauce into warm, dry sterilized bottles, holding the funnel up slightly from the neck to quicken the flow.
- Gently tap the bottom of the bottles on a hard surface to remove any air bubbles and seal.
- You can eat this one immediately or leave it to mature for 2–4 weeks before opening.

Keeps for up to 6 months to a year unopened. Once opened, keep in the fridge and eat within 4 months.

homemade brown sauce

The traditional brown sauce has been a staple in British homes since the 1800s. A bacon sandwich is not dressed without it. Try making it at home for a change—homemade always tastes better and you can give a bottle to your friends.

1¾ lbs apples
¾ lb red onions
1 garlic clove
¼ cup pitted dates
¼ cup pitted prunes
¾ cup water
2 cups white wine vinegar
1 cup apple juice
1 cup orange juice
1 cup tomato paste
1¼ cups tamarind paste
3 tbsp molasses
½ tsp whole cloves
½ tsp black peppercorns
½ tsp brown mustard seeds
½ tsp ground cardamom
½ tsp ground cinnamon
½ tsp onion powder
¾ tsp ground allspice
½ tsp cayenne pepper
1 tsp sea salt
⅔ cup cider vinegar

makes
2–3 x 17-ounce bottles

how to eat
in a breakfast bacon sandwich, of course

- Peel, core, and roughly chop the apples and peel and chop the onions. Peel and finely chop the garlic, dates, and prunes.
- In a large, lidded, heavy-bottomed pan or stock pot, combine the apples, onions, garlic, dates, prunes, water, white wine vinegar, apple and orange juices, tomato paste, tamarind paste, and molasses.
- Cover and bring the mixture to boil for 5 minutes.
- Uncover, reduce the heat and simmer, stirring intermittently, for 30–40 minutes until the fruit has softened. Remove from the heat and leave to cool then purée in a food processor or blender.
- Toast the cloves (see page 17), then put in a spice grinder with the peppercorns and mustard seeds and grind to a fine powder. Place in a bowl with the cardamom, cinnamon, onion powder, allspice, cayenne pepper, and salt. Slowly stir in the cider vinegar to make a paste.
- Put the blended fruit and white wine vinegar mixture in a large, heavy-bottomed pan, bring to boil, then slowly add the spice and cider vinegar paste.
- Mix thoroughly and simmer on a moderate heat, stirring intermittently, for another 30–40 minutes or until the sauce reduces and thickens to the desired consistency.
- Using a funnel, ladle or pour the sauce into warm, dry sterilized bottles.
- Gently tap the bottles against a hard surface to remove any air bubbles and seal.
- Can be eaten immediately but best left to mature for 2–4 weeks before opening.

Keeps for up to 6 months to a year unopened. Once opened, refrigerate and eat within 4 months.

pickles, fermentations, and vinegars

While writing this book I have been experimenting with pickling and I have learned a great deal. Pickling, fermentation, and making vinegars are major new trends among forward-thinking cooks around the world. But, although its modern exponents tend to be more experimental, it is born out of ancient roots.

Pickling is thought to date back thousands of years; it is even acclaimed in the Bible for its nutritional and health benefits! Fermentation has been around even longer and cooks have been making vinegars, alcohols, and soured vegetables since the Neolithic age. The recipes that follow are by no means the final word on this wonderful craft—and there are plenty of great books out there to help you learn—but I hope my recipes are a great start for anyone who wants to begin exploring.

pickles

Pickles are fruit or vegetables preserved by being immersed in brine.
They can be sweet or savory but are most definitely always sharp.
A pickle brine is usually a warmed blend of vinegar, sugar, and salt with
an infusion of different spices, and in some cases, citrus juice is added.

Pickles are a clever way to "save the season" and preserve raw, whole
food for a later date, and in the days before refrigeration, they were the
only way for people to keep their harvest beyond the summer into the
colder months. It is a joy to see a pantry full of pickles lined up in a row—
it's like seeing the seasons stored up, ready to be opened for a memory
of warmer weather on an unforgiving winter's day.

Pickles almost always need a maceration period of 4–8 weeks so that the
brines fully penetrate and preserve the fruit or vegetables. Having said
that, I have included some quick pickles that have a shorter maceration
period and those that can be eaten almost immediately, but they need
refrigeration and their shelf life is somewhat more limited.

fermentation

At first, I was scared to try fermentation; I was worried about messing
with yeasts and bacteria. But once I dove in I found it surprisingly easy and
satisfying. Fermentation is the metabolic process which turns
the natural sugars within fruits and vegetables into acids, gases, or alcohols.
The key ingredients are salts and sugars which, when added to the
produce, break down the fibers and release the sugars within controlled
temperatures. Time is also key; this metabolic transformation from raw to
pickled can take from a few days to a few months.

Fruit and vegetables have naturally high sugar levels so fermentation gently
decomposes the produce, allowing yeast and thousands of good bacteria
to transform it into a byproduct of either vinegar (acetic acid) or alcohol.
The vinegar that is created becomes its own "self-pickling" brine. Salt is
added as a preserve so that the produce fibers don't completely break
down. Sauerkraut (see page 108) is a great example of this: the cabbage
partially breaks down, and creates its own pickling vinegar after a few
weeks, while the added salt preserves its crunch.

Some forms of fermentation, such as gin distilling or beer brewing, break
down the fruit, vegetable, or grain to a greater extent, without added salts
to preserve any fibers, so the byproduct becomes alcohol. I don't really
go into this type of fermentation in this chapter, as a lot of equipment can
be needed, but I cover a similar, basic process with my recipe for homemade
vinegars made from fruit scraps (see page 104). As well as using these
vinegars to cook with in all the usual ways, some people swear by drinking

small quantities for the "good bacteria" they produce. If you are going to drink fruit vinegars, make sure it is in very small amounts—no more than a tablespoon—and not if you are pregnant or have any existing medical conditions.

It is not just vinegars that are considered good for you. Fermented products in general are thought to have health-giving properties. For one thing they are made from raw fruit or vegetables. It is also believed that the "good bacteria," which builds up during fermentation, placate the stomach and help digestion. Some people think it cures all sorts of diseases, but this theory is heavily debated and unproved.

key ingredients

Vinegar, salt, sugar, and spices are the classic ingredients you would expect to find in a pickle.

Vinegar: This is the main preserving agent for pickles. You can use a variety for different flavors, just make sure whatever you use contains at least 5 percent acetic acid content for long preservation. Rice and rice wine vinegars have a lower acetic acid level so they don't preserve food for as long as other vinegars.

Salt: This helps the yeast/bacteria to break down the cell walls of the vegetables to release the juices. In some pickling recipes you salt the vegetables overnight so they retain their crunch.

Sugar: You can vary the type of sugar you use to pickle in order to give different flavors. I tend to use plain white sugar, as opposed to brown and raw sugars, as their flavor can dominate.

Spices: These lend your pickles and ferments their different flavors. You add spices whole to pickle brines, then warm the brine to encourage the spices to infuse the vinegar with flavor. However, some recipes use a cold brine and then the spice flavor infuses over time.

key equipment

- Several large 1–3 liter, wide-rimmed glass jars with rubber-sealed lids: for storing pickles.
- A large, wide-rimmed 1–3 liter open jar: for fermentation, with a muslin cover/hat or, if you have one, a pottery crock (these tend to regulate the temperature more accurately while allowing air into the mixture, aiding the process).
- Medium, stainless steel pan: for brewing vinegar brines.
- Muddler/flat-ended rolling pin: important for pounding and breaking down the sugars in the fruit and vegetables when fermenting.
- Weighted object: While fermenting, the ingredients need pressure, to squash and compress them down into the jar or crock. This can be done by filling a plastic bag with cold water, sealing it tightly and placing it on top of a sterilized small plate that fits into the circumference of the vessel.
- Ladle, glass, or metal jug and a spatula: for pouring the brine into the jars and scraping out the remains.
- Mandoline: This is helpful for lots of shredding or slicing.

method tips

- Use fresh fruit and vegetables for pickling and fermentation. Use older over-ripe fruit and collected fruit scraps for making vinegars from scratch. Fruit that is starting to go moldy shouldn't be used, because it has already developed bacteria, but not the sort you want in your pickle! If only some of a piece of fruit has gone moldy, you can cut out the bad bits, and use what remains, but make sure to do this very carefully, not accidentally leaving mold and bad bacteria in the mixture.

- Chop the fruit and vegetables into similar-size dices, strips, or slices for an even pickle. Stack or put attractively into the jars.

- Always use sterilized jars, bottles, and lids (see page 13 for the method) for a longer preservation period. Don't pack the vegetables too tightly, to avoid bruising, and leave about $\frac{1}{3}$-inch at the top of the jar between the fill level and the lid. Always make sure the fruit and vegetables are completely covered with brine.

- Store in a cool, dark place for at least 4–8 weeks before using, unless the recipe states otherwise.

breaking the rules

Once you become familiar with a few of the general rules, you can pickle almost anything, so don't hesitate to have a try and play around with different spices, fruits, and vegetables. If you want an easy place to start, try making interesting flavored vinegars with fruits that are past their prime (see page 104).

pickled samphire

I discovered samphire (sea bean) about six years ago and until then I was completely unaware of its existence. Now I can't get enough of this salty delight. Buy it very fresh and pickle it immediately for best results. In the old days, sailors would take pickled samphire on long voyages to combat scurvy. You can find it at farmers' markets in coastal communities or forage it yourself by the beach.

2 cups white wine vinegar
½ cup granulated sugar
½ tsp cayenne pepper
½ tsp fennel seeds
1 tsp yellow mustard seeds
1 tsp black peppercorns
4 whole cloves
¾ lb samphire

makes
3 x 10-ounce jars or 1-liter jar

season midsummer, for about 2 months

how to eat
samphire is naturally salty and the vinegar makes it sharp, so eat with steamed white fish and potatoes with a good dollop of mayonnaise, preferably homemade

- In a medium, stainless steel pan, bring the vinegar, sugar, and spices to boil. Simmer for 5 minutes to let all the flavors infuse then remove and leave to cool completely.
- Prepare the samphire by blanching it in boiling water for 1½ minutes, then immediately dunk it into ice-cold water to stop it cooking. Drain and pat dry.
- Put the blanched samphire into warm, dry sterilized jars, cover with the spiced liquid and seal.
- You can eat this immediately or keep it sealed in a cool, dark cupboard for up to 4 weeks to let the flavors mature before opening.

Once opened, keep refrigerated and eat within 4 weeks.

pink pickled radishes

I first tried pickled radishes in a Middle Eastern restaurant with a mezze of dips, cold meats, and other pickles and immediately wanted to make my own version. I think these are pretty close. We often enjoy these as a light starter before a main meal.

2 cups cider vinegar
¾ cup granulated sugar
1 lime, zest and juice
1–2 slices raw peeled beets
2 bay leaves
½ tsp ground allspice
2 tsp white or pink peppercorns
1 tsp sea salt
2 lbs red radishes

makes
3–4 x 10-ounce jars

season midsummer to late autumn

how to eat
try with a mezze of dips (such as hummus and tzatziki), olives, and cold meats (such as salamis and other charcuterie) and other pickles

This recipe gets its color from the beets so, for best results, use raw beets.

- Put the vinegar and sugar in a medium, stainless steel pan and gently bring to a simmer, stirring intermittently until the sugar has dissolved.
- Add the lime zest and juice, beets, spices, and salt and leave to infuse on a gentle heat for at least 5 minutes.
- Remove from the heat and leave to cool while preparing the radishes.
- Trim the ends of the radishes, then slice into thin discs.
- Stack the radish slices into warm, dry sterilized jars, then cover with the pickling brine, distributing the spices evenly between the jars and pushing gently down on the stacks to remove any excess air.
- Tap the jars gently on a hard surface to remove any more air bubbles, check that the brine is just below the rim of the jar and add more if necessary, then seal.
- Keep sealed in a cool, dark place for at least 48 hours before eating.

Keeps for up to 6 months unopened. Once opened, keep in the fridge and eat within 4 weeks.

polish ćwikła (chee-kweh)

3½ lbs beets
1½ tsp granulated sugar
1 tbsp salt
½ cup distilled malt vinegar
1–1½ tbsp freshly ground
    black pepper (to taste)
1 cup fresh grated horseradish
    (to taste)
2–3 tbsp lemon juice

makes
4–5 x 10-ounce jars

how to eat
have a Polish Easter with a selection
of cold meats, egg salad, and a variety
of other Polish pickles

The trick here is first to boil the beets with their skins on as this keeps their vibrant color from escaping. Taste the ćwikła while you slowly add the horseradish until you get to your desired heat.

- Wash the beets, leaving the skins on, then cook in boiling water for about 10 minutes. They should still be firm to the touch. Drain, then peel and grate them finely and mix in a bowl with the sugar and salt.
- Add the vinegar and black pepper and mix thoroughly.
- Peel and finely grate the fresh horseradish until you get about 8–9 heaped tablespoons. Add this to the beets, little by little, tasting it as you go to get the desired kick.
- Stir through the lemon juice to taste, then spoon into warm, dry sterilized jars and seal.
- Eat immediately or store in the fridge sealed for up to 6 weeks.

Once opened, keep refrigerated and eat within 2 weeks.

za'atar pickled cauliflower

Za'atar is one of those Middle Eastern spice blends that has become ubiquitous in recent years. A mixture of dried herbs, spices, sesame seeds, and salt, it is a delicious condiment to perk up pickled cauliflower florets. Their sharp vinegary crunch is lovely in a salad.

1 ⅓ lbs cauliflower
6 pickling onions or shallots
2 ½ cups white wine vinegar
1 ¼ cups water
1 tsp pink peppercorns
1 tsp cumin seeds
1 ½ tbsp sea salt
1 ½ tsp granulated sugar
3 tsp za'atar

makes
6–7 x 10-ounce jars

how to eat
add to a green or couscous salad. Eat at the start of a meal with a selection of other pickles, dips, and cold meats

- Trim the cauliflower and break into florets. Peel and finely slice the onions or shallots.
- In a medium, stainless steel pan, combine the vinegar, water, peppercorns, cumin seeds, salt, and sugar. Bring gently to a simmer, dissolving the salt and sugar for about 5 minutes. Remove from the heat and allow to cool completely for 5–10 minutes.
- Put ¾ tsp za'atar in the bottom of each warm, dry sterilized jar, then pack with the florets and the sliced onions until they are ⅓-inches from the rim.
- Pour in the brine, distributing the peppercorns and cumin seeds evenly, and leave ¼ inch between the fill level and the top of the jar.
- Tap the jars gently on a hard surface to remove any air bubbles and top up with more liquid if the level has dropped more than ¼ inch below the rim. Seal.
- Keep sealed in a cool, dark place for at least 4 weeks to allow the florets to pickle, turning the jars intermittently to distribute the spices throughout.

Keeps for up to a year. Eat within 4 weeks once opened and keep refrigerated.

pickled onions

I've always been unsure about fishing this English classic out from those giant jars placed on the bar of my local pub. But this recipe is a safe bet! Perk up your all-American lunch with a few of these tart little numbers. They are also very easy to make, especially with my tips on peeling the little devils.

3⅓ lbs pickling onions or baby
    round shallots
5 tsp salt
4¼ cups distilled malt vinegar
1 cup granulated sugar
2 tsp chili flakes
½ tsp fennel seeds
½ tsp coriander seeds
1 tsp yellow mustard seeds
1 tsp black peppercorns

makes
2–3 x 17-ounce jars

how to eat
a national classic in pubs. Eat by themselves or in a meaty sandwich

Choose the smallest baby onions or shallots you can get your hands on. To peel the onions, trim them, put them in a heatproof bowl, and cover them in boiling water. Let the water cool down and then drain so the onions don't get too soft. Rub off the skins, rinse, and dry.

- Put the onions in a bowl and sprinkle the salt over them, making sure they are all evenly covered. Leave overnight but no longer than 24 hours or else they will soften and not have their desired crunch.
- Put all of the remaining ingredients into a medium, stainless steel pan and gently heat without boiling, dissolving the sugar and infusing the spices for 5 minutes. Remove from the heat, cool the liquid and refrigerate overnight.
- The next day, rinse the salt off the onions and completely dry them with kitchen paper.
- Put the onions into warm, dry sterilized jars, cover with the spiced vinegar brine and seal.
- Leave to mature sealed in a cool, dark cupboard for at least 1 week, if you can wait, but they will be even better after 4 weeks.

Keeps for up to a year. Once opened, refrigerate and eat within 4 weeks.

gin pickled cucumber

This has to be one of my biggest sellers in the summer. People love the idea of gin, mint, and cucumber on ice with a dash of tonic, and this recipe mixes this idea up, making the cucumber the headliner for a change, not the gin. We love these on a buttermilk-fried chicken burger, or used to garnish the edge of a gin martini glass instead of an olive.

1 Thai chili
1 lime, zest and juice
2 cups white wine vinegar
1 tbsp granulated sugar
1½ tsp sea salt
12–15 juniper berries (3 in each jar)
1–2 large cucumbers
8 baby round shallots
2–3 sprigs fresh mint
⅓–½ cup gin (1¾ tbsp per jar)

makes
4–5 x 10-ounce jars

how to eat
these are sharp, boozy, and spicy.
Try with chicken, fish, or beef burgers.
They are also great with smoked/
steamed/baked salmon or trout
or simply spice up your work lunch
sandwich with a few

If you prefer these without a chili kick, deseed the chili for a milder flavour.

- Finely chop the chili (and deseed if you like) and put in a medium, stainless steel saucepan with the lime zest and juice, vinegar, sugar, salt, and juniper berries.
- Bring to a gentle simmer, dissolving the sugar and infusing the flavors for around 5 minutes.
- Remove from the heat and leave to cool while you prepare the other ingredients.
- Finely slice the cucumbers—a mandoline does this perfectly but you can slice them with a knife if you don't have one or prefer thicker slices. Peel and finely slice the shallots Strip the mint leaves from the stalks.
- Start by stacking layers of cucumber, shallot, and mint into warm, dry sterilized jars until the jars are half-full.
- Add 1¾ tablespoons gin and 2 juniper berries (from the vinegar brine) to each jar and continue to stack, until the vegetables are about ⅓ inch below the rim.
- Fill the jars with the vinegar brine, distributing the remaining spices (in the brine) evenly between them and gently pushing down on the contents to let the air bubbles out. Tap the jars gently on a hard surface to remove any more bubbles, add more brine if necessary to completely cover the vegetables, then seal.
- Eat the next day if you like a crunch to your pickle, or keep sealed for up to 4 weeks in a cool, dark place to allow the flavors to marry.

Keeps for up to 6 months unopened. Once opened, refrigerate and eat within 4 weeks.

pickled cucumber relish

This recipe is easy and can be eaten almost immediately. It won't keep for as long as other pickles so store it in the fridge from day one. It makes a clean, fresh-tasting accompaniment to a wholesome summer meal like grilled or steamed fish and salad.

2 medium cucumbers
1½ tbsp salt
ice cubes
1 small red onion
1 large red pepper
1 long chili (red or green)
½ cup white wine vinegar
½ tsp coriander seeds
¼ tsp fennel seeds
½ tsp ground ginger
¼ tsp ground allspice
1 cup granulated sugar

makes
2 x 10-ounce jars

season summer to spring

how to eat
with corn or green vegetable fritters, or on top of ceviche or grilled white fish

It's best to pulse the vegetables lightly in a food processor 7 or 8 times, making sure they don't go mushy. If you don't have a food processor, take the time to finely chop them into uniform pieces.

- Trim the cucumbers, then chop into pieces. Put in a large bowl, sprinkle with the salt, then cover with ice cubes. Leave for 8 hours or overnight; this helps to drain the excess moisture from the cucumbers.
- The next day, drain and dry the cucumber with kitchen paper.
- Peel and finely chop the onion, finely chop the red pepper and chili then pulse-blend them together with the cucumber. Transfer to a large bowl.
- Warm the vinegar in a medium, stainless steel pan and, while it warms, blend or crush the spices together, then add these to the vinegar.
- Bring to a gentle simmer to infuse for about 5 minutes, then add the sugar and stir until it has dissolved.
- Drain any excess liquid from the vegetables and mix with the spiced vinegar brine.
- Spoon into warm, dry sterilized jars, filling them to about ¼ inch below the rim and seal.

Keep in the fridge and eat immediately, but can be stored sealed in the fridge for up to 4 weeks. Once opened, eat within 1 week.

pickled jalapeños

Impress your friends with homemade pickled jalapeños on nachos, pizza, or even just cheese on toast.

1 lb jalapeños
1¼ cups cider vinegar
1¼ cups water
1½ tbsp granulated sugar

for each jar
¼ tsp cumin seeds
½ garlic clove, peeled
1 bay leaf
½ tsp salt
¼ tsp freshly ground black pepper

makes
6–7 x 10-ounce jars

season summer to spring

how to eat
with nachos, pizza, or cheese on toast

If you don't have cider vinegar, use distilled malt vinegar or a combination of both. Honey can be substituted for the sugar.

- Finely slice the jalapeños crossways into 1–1½ inch pieces. Warm the vinegar, water, and sugar in a medium, stainless steel pan, until the sugar dissolves. Bring to a simmer but don't let it boil.
- Put the spices and seasonings into warm, dry sterilized jars, then stack the jalapeño slices on top, gently pressing them down and packing them in tightly, until the jars are filled to about ¼ inch below the rim.
- Pour the warm vinegar brine into the jars, completely submerging the chilis and, again, filling them to about ¼ inch below the rim, then seal.
- Leave to marinate for at least 3 days before eating but if you can wait, then store sealed in a cool, dark cupboard for up to 4 weeks.

Once opened, keep in the fridge and eat within 4 weeks.

salt and pepper kumquats

Have you ever eaten preserved lemons or made them? Why not step it up a notch by trying this fun variation? Kumquats can be preserved in the same way and their unique flavor will liven up salads, couscous, or any other dish where you might normally use preserved lemons.

2 lbs kumquats
1 tbsp freshly ground black pepper
4 tbsp sea salt
¾ tsp ground cinnamon
3 lemons, zest only
1 ½ tbsp golden granulated sugar
about 1 ¼ cups of lemon juice
    (4–5 lemons)

makes
3–4 x 10-ounce jars or 1-liter jar

how to eat
slice up and use in salads or tagines
as you would a preserved lemon

- Make sure the kumquat skins are clean and completely dry (you will be using the whole fruit). Slice off the knobbly end and cut lengthwise (the seeds are edible). Toss in a bowl with the pepper, salt, cinnamon, lemon zest, and sugar until they are well coated.
- Put the kumquats into warm, dry sterilized jars, then pour in the lemon juice so that each jar is three-quarters full and seal.
- Store at room temperature and shake gently every day, to distribute the liquid evenly in the jars, for up to 2 weeks.
- They will soften in the jars over time, and the liquid will increase, but, as they have thinner skins than lemons, keep an eye on them to make sure that they are not starting to break apart inside the jars. If they are, then put them in the fridge to stop them fermenting any further.
- After the maceration period, store in the fridge for up to a year unopened.

Once opened, keep refrigerated and eat within 4–6 weeks.

fennel and orange pickle

The beautiful thing about fennel is that it can be used "nose to tail." You can use the stalks and leaves as an herb, the seeds as a spice, and the bulb as a vegetable. It is characterized by its strong aniseed flavor and this recipe celebrates that by matching it with notes of orange. This is a delight when served with a whole fish, wrapped in foil, and baked. Try it with tilapia, cod, or haddock.

3 fennel bulbs
4 Thai chilis
1¾ cups cider vinegar
¾ cup water
3 tbsp raw granulated sugar
2 oranges, zest only
½ lemon, zest only
1½ tsp yellow mustard seeds
1 tsp chili flakes
½ tsp black peppercorns
1½ tsp sea salt
8–10 fennel leaves (reserved from fennel above)

makes
3 x 10-ounce jars

season spring to early autumn

how to eat
with a mozzarella or burrata salad or serve as a condiment with whole-steamed white fish

- Prepare the fennel bulbs by trimming the ends, cutting off the stalks and keeping some leaves for garnish. Finely slice the bulbs, either with a mandoline or sharp knife. Finely chop (and deseed if you like) the chilis.
- Combine all of the remaining ingredients (including the chopped chilis), except any reserved fennel leaves, in a medium, stainless steel pan and bring to a simmer for about 5 minutes, until the sugar has dissolved and the spices have infused.
- Remove from the heat and leave to cool slightly.
- Tightly pack the fennel slices into warm, dry sterilized jars ⅓ inch from the rim then pour in the brine, distributing the spices evenly.
- Fill the jars to about ¼ inch below the rim, then gently tap the jars to remove any air bubbles. Top up with brine if necessary.
- Add a couple of the reserved fennel leaves to each jar and seal.
- Can be eaten within a few days or store sealed in a cool, dark place for 3 weeks to marinate.

Keeps for up to 4-6 months unopened. Once opened, keep in the fridge and eat within 4 weeks.

posh piccalilli

I call this posh piccalilli because I love to add heirloom vegetables, such as purple, yellow, and red carrots to the mix. You can also use romanesco, broccoli, daikon radish, or podded peas for extra color and crunch—experiment to make a gorgeously vibrant pickle.

2½ lbs selection of 6 vegetables: cauliflower, romanesco, daikon radish, zucchini, cucumber, green beans, fresh peas, heritage carrots, shallots, red/yellow/ green peppers, fresh corn kernels
2 tbsp salt
1 tsp coriander seeds
1 tsp cumin seeds
1 tbsp yellow mustard seeds
2½ tbsp cornflour
2 tsp ground turmeric
2 tsp yellow mustard powder
3 cups cider vinegar
½ cup granulated sugar
4 tbsp honey

makes
6–7 x 10-ounce jars

how to eat
an Anglo-Indian classic—eat with cheddar on crackers or in a sandwich

The key to this recipe is to dry the salted vegetables thoroughly so excess water doesn't ruin the thickened sauce once in the jars.

- Prepare the vegetables by cutting them into small, similar-size pieces (about 1 inch each is ideal). Put in a bowl, sprinkle with the salt, making sure it is evenly distributed, and leave at room temperature for at least 24 hours.
- The next day, rinse the vegetables with ice-cold water, drain and dry thoroughly, either in a salad spinner if you have one, or by patting dry with kitchen paper.
- Blend or crush together the coriander, cumin, and mustard seeds. Put in a bowl with the cornflour, turmeric, and mustard powder, then stir in a little of the vinegar to make a paste.
- Bring the remainder of the vinegar, the sugar, and honey to a gentle simmer in a medium, stainless steel pan, slowly dissolving the sugar.
- Add a ladle of this warmed vinegar to the spice paste and mix well.
- Slowly pour this sloppy paste into the pan of vinegar on the heat, stirring as you pour.
- Bring to a simmer, stirring, allowing the cornflour to thicken the mixture until it is a bit like a thick pancake batter.
- Remove from the heat, add the dry vegetables, and stir until well coated with the mixture.
- Pack the piccalilli into warm, dry sterilized jars, filling them to about ¼ inch below the rim and seal.
- Can be eaten immediately but is best kept sealed in a cool, dark place for 3–4 weeks to allow the spices to infuse into the vegetables and for the sharpness of the vinegar to mellow.

Keeps unopened for up to a year. Once opened, keep refrigerated and eat within 4 weeks.

spicy beer or bourbon pickles

These New York-style pickled cucumbers, a bit like gherkins, are great for barbecues and burgers but are also good enough to eat straight from the jar. Cucumbers absorb other flavors really well so they make the perfect ingredient for pickling with booze, such as a local craft beer or a good bourbon whiskey.

2½ lbs small pickling cucumbers
1 garlic clove
½ cup local craft beer or
   a bourbon whiskey
⅓ cup water
¾ cup cider vinegar
¾ cup raw sugar
1 tbsp yellow mustard seeds
1 tbsp black peppercorns
1 tbsp sea salt
½ tsp chili flakes, or to taste

makes
4 x 8-ounce tall jars

how to eat
on a grilled cheese, mixed through a potato salad with bacon, in a burger, with cheese and crackers... the list goes on!

- Trim the ends of the cucumbers and cut lengthwise into quarters. Peel and finely chop the garlic.
- Prepare the brine by combining the rest of the ingredients, along with the garlic, in a medium, stainless steel pan, then bring the liquid to a simmer, stirring gently to dissolve the sugar and salt. Remove from the heat and leave to cool.
- Collect the cucumber quarters into one big vertical bunch and pack them lengthwise (upright) into warm, dry sterilized jars.
- Pour in the cooled brine to fill the jars to about ¼ inch below the rim. Tap the jars gently to remove any air bubbles and top up with brine if necessary.
- Seal and store in the fridge for at least 2–4 days before eating to allow the flavors to permeate.

Keeps for up to 4 months in the fridge unopened. Once opened, keep refrigerated and eat within 4 weeks.

pickled green beans

Having a jar of these in the fridge is a must for weekend hair-of-the-dog moments. These hot little beans can sort out any hangover, especially when added to a Bloody Mary . . .

1 lb green beans
4 Thai chilis
1 garlic clove
1 ¼ cups cider vinegar
1 cup water
1 tsp honey
2 bay leaves
¾ tsp white peppercorns
1 tsp allspice berries
½ tsp coriander seeds
½ tsp chili flakes
1 tsp sea salt

makes
1-liter jar

how to eat
in a Bloody Mary as an alternative
to a celery stick

- Trim the ends of the green beans, then blanch them in boiling water for 3 minutes. Remove from the pan and quickly dunk them in ice-cold water to stop them cooking. Drain and dry. Finely slice the chilis, deseeding them if you prefer less spicy pickles. Peel the garlic but leave it whole.
- Put the chilis, vinegar, water, honey, and all the seasonings and spices in a medium, stainless steel pan and bring to a boil. Reduce the heat and simmer gently for 5 minutes.
- Bunch your green beans up (lengthwise, as if they were flower stems), then put them into a warm, dry sterilized jar. Add the garlic clove and pour in the brine, filling the jar to about ¼ inch below the rim and seal.
- Leave to marinate in a cool, dark place for at least 1 week before opening and eating.

Keeps for up to a year unopened. Once opened, refrigerate and eat within 4 weeks.

japanese pickle brine

This simple Japanese-inspired recipe makes a brilliant brine for pickles. I have used it as the basis for various recipes to follow, but you can combine it with several different fruits or vegetables. Rice wine vinegar, a slightly sweeter and less tart vinegar, makes a gentle flavored brine, more palatable for those who don't like the sharp vinegar burst that other pickles have. However, because it has a lower acetic acid level, it doesn't preserve as long as other vinegars, so keep this in mind.

2 cups rice wine vinegar
2 cups water
2 cups superfine granulated sugar
$\frac{1}{4}$ tsp sea salt
$\frac{1}{2}$ tsp black or white peppercorns

makes
1-liter jar

Can be made days ahead and kept in the fridge until ready to use. Halve the recipe if you require less brine.

- Put all of the ingredients into a medium, stainless steel pan and warm the mixture until the sugar has dissolved. Bring to a simmer and infuse for 2–3 minutes. Set aside to cool before use or storing.

japanese pickled ginger

I love Japanese food—it is both light and filling and should always be eaten with a serving of pickled ginger on the side.

$\frac{3}{4}$ cup fresh ginger
1 tsp salt
$1\frac{1}{4}$ cups Japanese Pickle Brine (see above)

makes
4 x 3-ounce jars or 1 x 12-ounce jar

how to eat
with sashimi, sushi, rice and salmon, or add to fruit before stewing for a bit of spice

- Peel the ginger and slice as finely as possible into long ribbons, either using a vegetable peeler or a mandoline.
- In a bowl, cover the ginger with the salt and mix together with your hands to make sure the ginger is completely covered. Set aside for 30–40 minutes.
- The salt extracts liquid from the ginger so, after the allotted time, carefully squeeze it to remove any excess salted liquid and put into warm, dry sterilized jars.
- Gently warm the brine, pour over the ginger, filling the jars to about $\frac{1}{4}$ inch below the rim, then seal.
- Leave in the fridge to macerate for 24 hours so the flavors develop before eating.

Keeps unopened in the fridge for up to 6 months. Once opened, eat within 4 weeks.

heirloom carrot and ginger pickle

I like using heirloom vegetables in recipes because they are reminiscent of the past. And, apart from that, I love their color. Here I use yellow carrots with ginger to add both life and spice to any salad. A nutritious and visual feast.

⅓ cup fresh ginger
½ lb yellow heirloom carrots
2 tsp salt
2½–3 cups Japanese Pickle Brine
(see page 93)

makes
about 3 x 10-ounce jars or 1-liter jar

how to eat
add to a shredded Japanese salad of cucumber and sesame seeds, or eat straight from the jar

- Peel and trim the ginger and carrots, then slice as finely as possible into long ribbons, using a vegetable peeler or a mandoline.
- Put the ginger with ½ teaspoon of salt in a bowl and mix with your hands to make sure it is completely covered. In a separate bowl, mix the carrots with the remaining 1½ teaspoons of salt, again using your hands to make sure they are completely covered. Set both aside for 30–40 minutes.
- Gently squeeze the ginger and the carrot ribbons to remove any excess salted liquid, combine the ribbons in a bowl then pack into warm, dry sterilized jars.
- Gently warm the brine and pour over the ginger and carrots, filling the jars to about ¼ inch below the rim then seal.
- Leave in the fridge to macerate for 24 hours so the flavors develop before eating.

  Keeps unopened in the fridge for up to 6 months. Once opened, eat within 4 weeks.

preserved lemons with rosemary

Preserving lemons in Japanese brine, rather than in the classic Moroccan style, gives them an Asian nuance that works surprisingly well in the context of traditional Middle Eastern dishes like tagines. Unlike salt-preserved lemons, these rosemary-scented ones are also perfect for using in puddings thanks to their sweeter brine.

4 lemons
8–12 1 inch sprigs fresh rosemary
1½–2½ cups Japanese Pickle Brine
    (see page 93)

makes
4 x 8–8.5 ounce jars or 1-liter jar

how to eat
use as you would any other preserved lemons. Try finely chopping them and adding them to your favorite dessert or pastry

- Trim the ends of the lemons, then cut them first into quarters and then into eighths. If you are using a liter jar, just chop the lemons into quarters instead.
- Fill your jars with the lemon pieces and put 2 or 3 sprigs of rosemary down the sides of each jar.
- Gently warm the brine, then pour it into the jars to fill them to about ¼ inch below the rim.
- Tap the filled jars gently to remove any air bubbles, top up with the brine, then seal.
- Allow the flavors to develop for 10–14 days before eating, gently agitating the jars from time to time.

Keeps unopened for up to 6–8 months in a cool, dark cupboard. Once opened, refrigerate and eat within 4 weeks.

pickled daikon with lemon thyme

Here the Japanese brine balances the flavor of the daikon so this pickle adds a sweet, peppery crunch to a meal. The interestingly shaped daikon is actually a long white radish. It looks fantastic in a jar so it makes for a delightful gift.

1 whole daikon radish
6 sprigs fresh lemon thyme
2½–3 cups Japanese Pickle Brine
(see page 93)

makes
about 3 x 10-ounce jars or 1-liter jar

how to eat
add a crunch and texture to rice dishes such as Japanese curry with rice. Or use instead of kimchi or sauerkraut

- Peel, then carefully slice the daikon into fine discs with a mandoline or sharp knife, then rinse and dry completely. Set aside.
- Pluck the leaves from the sprigs of lemon thyme, leaving some of the smaller-leaved stalks intact.
- Layer the daikon slices with the lemon thyme, both leaves and sprigs, and add the peppercorns from the brine, into warm, dry sterilized jars, distributing the spices evenly.
- Gently warm the brine and pour into the jars, filling them to about ¼ inch below the rim.
- Tap the filled jars gently to remove any air bubbles and seal.
- Leave in the fridge to macerate for 24 hours so the flavors develop before eating.

Keeps unopened in the fridge for up to 6 months. Once opened, eat within 4 weeks.

shallots pickled with lavender

This is an upmarket twist on the Pickled Onions (see page 75) where Japan meets Provence. Shallots have a particular natural sweetness that is enhanced by the floral notes of lavender. You can add more or less lavender according to taste.

1 lb small round shallots or pickling onions
1½ tsp edible lavender flowers
1¾–2 cups Japanese Pickle Brine (see page 93)

makes
about 3 x 10-ounce jars or 1-liter jar

how to eat
mixed through a potato salad, or on a burger. Eat with cheese or with a mezze of cold meats, pickles, and dips

- Prepare the shallots first by chopping off the root ends, submerging them in boiling water for 1 minute, and then quickly dunking them in ice water for another minute. The skins should slip off easily.
- Cut the shallots lengthwise and separate the layers into their individual petals.
- Put ½ teaspoon of the lavender flowers into the bottom of each warm, dry sterilized jar or, if just using one jar, add it all.
- Evenly distribute the shallot petals between the jars.
- Gently warm the brine, then pour over the shallots, filling the jars to about ¼ inch below the rim. Tap the jars gently to remove any air bubbles, top up with brine if necessary, then seal.
- Leave to macerate in the fridge for 24 hours so the flavors develop before eating.

Keeps unopened in the fridge for up to 6 months. Once opened, eat within 4 weeks.

~473ml

475 ml

fermented fruit vinegar

Making vinegar out of fermented fruit and vegetables is a great way to avoid food waste. You can make fruit vinegar from most fruit, be it strawberries, apples, or sweeter stone fruits. All you need are the leftover scraps, water, and a little sugar—it really is that simple. Try this recipe with the cores and peels of apples or pears, the stems of hulled strawberries, or over-ripe soft fruit like peaches, pears, plums, or grapes. But avoid citrus fruits: because they contain less sugar, they don't break down in the same way and so don't transform like the more sugar-heavy fruits.

Homemade vinegars are a fun way to add interest to ordinary dressings. For example, try sprinkling strawberry vinegar straight over mixed greens for a touch of summer on your plate. These vinegars are best eaten fresh, so they are not suitable for pickling or cooking in a chutney.

about 10 apples, scraps, cores, peel (this makes about 1¾ cups scraps measured in a jug—see below)
3 tbsp granulated sugar
3½ cups lukewarm water (heated to about 86–104°F)
splash of cider vinegar

makes
depends on the amount of fruit scraps you start with but make sure you have about 3–4 8.5-ounce bottles prepared just in case

how to eat
add it to your favorite dressings or just pour straight onto salad leaves. If you are after the health benefits of vinegar, drink it as a shot for breakfast or before bedtime as a means of adding nutrients and minerals to your diet

You can double or halve this recipe depending on your quantity of fruit—simply adjust the ratios of sugar and water in proportion. You should have 1 part fruit scraps to 2 parts sugar-water mix. Measure your scraps in a measuring cup, reading the height they reach in the cup. If you have 2 cups of scraps you will need 1 liter (4 cups) of sugar/water mix.

- Put the scraps in your widest-based, food-safe glass container, something that can deal with high acidity levels (so not some plastics or some metals).
- Measure out the scraps, sugar, and water as detailed above, then dissolve the sugar in the lukewarm water and pour over your scraps. Make up more liquid if needed until the scraps are generously submerged.
- Cover the container with a muslin square, secure with string or an elastic band and let the mixture sit in a dark cupboard, swirling it daily, for about 1 week.
- A good fermentation temperature is on the warmer end of 79–82°F. If it's cooler, it is not a problem; it will just take longer to ferment.
- After a week the mixture should start bubbling. This means bacteria and wild yeasts are eating the sugars, thus producing the desired carbon dioxide, and fermentation is in process.

- Strain through a muslin-lined, fine metal sieve to separate the liquid and scraps. Discard the scraps.
- Clean and dry the food-safe container you used for the fermentation, then add the strained liquid and a splash of cider vinegar, either from the cupboard, or use a bit of the "mother" you collect at a later stage of this process (see below).
- Cover and tie again with the muslin square and return to the warm, dark cupboard for 2–3 weeks, this time swirling very gently every other day in order not to disturb the growth that starts to form.
- After this period it should start to taste like vinegar and a "mother"—a bacterial slippery growth—should have formed. Remove the growth gently, wash in warm water and store it in a separate muslin-covered vessel with a bit of your newly made vinegar. This is handy for jumpstarting the process the next time you make vinegar.
- Strain the liquid again, this time through a fine-mesh sieve lined with a double layer of muslin, then pour the vinegar into warm, dry sterilized bottles and seal.

Keeps indefinitely in a cool, dry cupboard and matures, in depth of flavor, with age.

pickled baby beets

If you like goat cheese salads this is the recipe for you. It takes at least a few days to marinade to perfection but it is worth the wait. This is a classic example of how taking the time to pickle today makes for a tastier tomorrow.

1½ lbs baby beets
1¼ cups white wine vinegar
1 cup granulated sugar
2 tsp salt
1½ tsp whole cloves

makes
2 x 17-ounce jars or 1-liter jar

how to eat
sliced onto a burger, in a goat cheese, rocket, and pine nut salad or straight out of the jar. My Eastern European friends like to add these pickles to soups

- Wash the baby beets thoroughly, scrubbing off any dirt but keeping their skins on (to preserve their color). Cover with water in a pan, then bring to boil, cooking for around 7–10 minutes until they are tender to the touch.
- Drain, keeping ½ cup of the beet water. Leave to cool, then peel off the skins.
- Combine the reserved beet water, the vinegar, sugar, and salt in a medium, stainless steel pan, then gently bring to a simmer for about 5 minutes, making sure the sugar has dissolved.
- Divide the cloves equally between warm, dry sterilized jars, fill with the beet, then pour in the hot brine to about ¼ inch below the rim and seal.
- Can be eaten after 3 days but best left to marinate sealed for at least 3 weeks before eating.

Keeps unopened for up to a year. Once opened, refrigerate and eat within 4–6 weeks.

fermented lime pickle

If you enjoy making curries at home from scratch, then why not try and make the condiments to match? Anyone who likes a good Indian curry knows that lime pickle is a must... home-made is even better!

fermentation stage
1 lb limes, about 10 large
2½ tbsp salt
1 tbsp ground turmeric
1½ tbsp white wine vinegar

spice-developing stage
3 tbsp olive oil
½ tbsp asafoetida
1½ tbsp mustard seeds
¾ tbsp fenugreek seeds
1 tsp cumin seeds
1 tsp coriander seeds
¾ tsp chili powder, or to taste
½ cup water
¾ cup light brown sugar
1½ tbsp white wine vinegar

makes
about 3 x 10-ounce jars or 1-liter jar

how to eat
with curry of course. Or as a quick snack with papadums or naan bread

This recipe can take up to 5–6 weeks before you can eat. You need a large, wide-rimmed 2–3 liter jar or fermentation vessel to begin this recipe, as well as a large muddler or a flat-ended rolling pin.

- Trim the ends of the limes, then cut into eighths.
- Put all of the limes in a large bowl and sprinkle on the salt, turmeric, and 1½ tablespoons of vinegar. Mix together thoroughly and put in the large jar or vessel. Cover with a muslin square or a tea towel and secure.
- Let this mixture ferment for up to 4 weeks, opening the vessel every few days to muddle and stir gently and check the progression.
- After 4 weeks, and/or once the lime skins have softened, warm the olive oil gently in a pan on a low heat.
- Blend all of the spices, or crush them using a mortar and pestle, then stir into the warmed oil, letting them infuse for 5 minutes off the heat.
- Put the water, sugar, and remaining vinegar into a separate pan and simmer for about 5 minutes or until the sugar has dissolved.
- Slowly add the water mix to the spice mix, stirring constantly until well combined, then bring to boil and gently simmer for 10 minutes.
- Remove from the heat and leave to cool then add to the limes in the fermenting jar or vessel.
- Scrape down the inside of the vessel with a spatula, so that there are no spices or limes above the liquid level, then re-cover with the muslin and let sit for a further 10–14 days, stirring every couple of days to help the flavours to merge and develop.
- Once ready, spoon into warm, dry sterilized jars and seal.

Keeps for up to a year unopened. Once opened, refrigerate and eat within 6 weeks.

red cabbage sauerkraut

Cabbage is incredibly good for you, especially in its raw fermented state. It is high in vitamin C and is believed to placate stomach complaints and ulcers. This is a good recipe to make if you are new to fermentation. It takes a few weeks but it is easy and delicious. I prefer to use red cabbage in my sauerkraut as it has more vitamin C than green cabbage and it just looks prettier.

1 red cabbage
1 tbsp salt
1 apple
½ tsp chili flakes
¾ tsp juniper berries
1 tbsp caraway seeds

makes
4 x 8-ounce jars or 1-liter jar

how to eat
with a rye bread pastrami sandwich and lots of wholegrain mustard. But also try it warm, with wild game such as venison or boar

You don't have to own a pottery crock to make this recipe; use a 3-liter jar with a large opening instead. A large muddler or a flat-ended rolling pin is also helpful.

- Remove the outer leaves of the cabbage then cut it in half and slice it into ribbons ¼ inch wide. Put in a bowl and toss with the salt. Leave for 1 hour until the cabbage starts to sweat.
- Peel, core, and grate the apple and stir through the cabbage with the chili flakes, juniper berries, and caraway seeds.
- Put the mixture into a large 3-liter jar, along with any liquid from the bowl.
- With a muddler, rolling pin or any other long, flat-ended implement, push down on and compress the mixture until liquid starts to pool in the jar.
- Put something heavy on top of the cabbage, to keep it compressed while it rests. You can use a slightly smaller jar that fits inside the larger one or a plastic bag filled with water and sealed tightly.
- Over the next hour or two, intermittently remove the weight and pound/muddle the mixture, drawing out as much liquid as you can until it starts to cover the cabbage by about ⅓ inch.
- With a spatula, scrape the inside of the jar to push down any stray bits of cabbage under the level of the liquid.
- Return the weighted object to the jar, cover with a muslin square or clean tea towel, secure, then leave in a warm, dark place for 2–3 weeks.
- Fermentation should start in about 10–15 days, so sample it every few days.
- Once you have the desired tangy flavor, spoon it into warm, dry sterilized jars, seal, and store in the fridge for up to 4 months. Once opened, keep refrigerated and eat within 3 weeks.

kimchi

Korean-fermented vegetables, known as kimchi, are generally served as an accompaniment to a variety of traditional Korean meat, fish, and vegetable dishes. Like sauerkraut, kimchi is thought to have health-giving properties because of its combination of raw super-food vegetables and the "good" bacteria produced during fermentation. More and more people are experimenting with making kimchi these days and you're as likely to find it in a street-food wrap or a burger as you would served alongside traditional Korean fare.

4 cups water

4 tbsp sea salt

1 firm cabbage (napa is traditional)

3 carrots

1 daikon

1 small onion

2 garlic cloves

2-inch piece fresh ginger

3 shallots

1 tbsp gochugaru powder or cayenne pepper

1 tbsp sea salt (optional)

**makes
about 4 x 10-ounce jars**

how to eat
with Korean marinated meats for your own Korean barbecue

Kimchi can take a few goes to get it right. My tips are: 1) Use sea salt that is unrefined because iodized salt will prevent your vegetables from fermenting. 2) Use a large glass jar with a wide opening or a ceramic fermentation pot, so the high salt content won't eat away at the vessel. 3) Use a hard cabbage that won't turn to mush. 4) Go easy on the aromatics such as garlic, onion, and ginger because these flavors increase during fermentation.

- Mix together the water and salt until the salt dissolves.
- Coarsely chop the cabbage. Peel the carrots and daikon and slice into fine discs using a mandoline, or make 2-inch-long ribbons using a vegetable peeler.
- Put the vegetables in a large bowl and cover in the salted brine.
- Soak for 8–24 hours, making sure the vegetables are completely covered with the liquid and put a plate on top of them to weigh the mixture down.
- Peel and dice the onion, garlic, ginger, and shallots, then put the onion, garlic, and ginger into a food processor or a mortar and pestle and blend/bash into a paste.
- Put the paste into a bowl and stir through the gochugaru powder and shallots.
- Drain the vegetables, reserving the brine. Taste the vegetables for saltiness. If they are too salty, rinse them with cold water; if they are not salty enough, mix through some extra sea salt.

(Recipe continues on page 114)

kimchi continued

- Combine the vegetables with the paste, mixing them well to ensure that they are evenly coated.
- Gently squeeze the vegetables with your hands. This bruises the cell walls and helps release their juices.
- Pack the mixture tightly into the bottom of a 2.5–3 liter glass jar or ceramic pot, gently pushing down with your fist to release more juice until it is submerged in its own liquid. If necessary, add some of the reserved brine just to cover.
- Scrape down and clean the inside of the jar with a spatula, then weigh the mixture down with a flat plate that fits inside the jar, with a weight on top (like a smaller jar filled with water and sealed).
- Cover the jar with a muslin square or tea towel so it can breathe, and secure.
- Leave to ferment in a warm place at around 68–77°F. If it's cooler, then it will just take longer.
- Check and taste daily, making sure the vegetables are always submerged in the brine. Depending on your taste and the room temperature, this can take around 3–14 days. It's ready when it tastes sour and tangy.
- Pack tightly into warm, dry sterilized jars leaving a ¼ inch gap between the top of the vegetables and the rim and seal.

Keeps for up to 6–8 months unopened in a cool, dark cupboard. Once opened, keep in the fridge and eat within 4–6 weeks.

pickled persimmons

Persimmons or sharon fruit are deliciously sweet. Once pickled, use them on savory or sweet hor d'oeuvres at dinner parties, or add to a green salad with toasted seeds and nuts.

4 persimmons
¾ cup white wine vinegar
½ cup rice wine vinegar
¾ cup raw sugar
1 tbsp grated fresh ginger
¼ tsp chili flakes
a pinch of saffron strands
1 tbsp sea salt

makes
3–4 x 8-ounce jars or 1-liter jar

season late summer to late autumn

how to eat
in a salad, on top of blintz with mascarpone, and a ham and cheese sandwich, or straight from the jar as a midnight snack

- Trim the ends of the persimmons and peel off the skins. Slice into ⅓-inch-thick discs, then cut each disc into 6 wedges.
- Put the rest of the ingredients in a medium, stainless steel pan and bring to a gentle simmer, stirring to dissolve the sugar and salt.
- Pack the persimmon wedges into warm, dry sterilized jars, then pour in the warm brine to fill to about ¼ inch below the rim.
- Gently tap out any air bubbles and top up with more brine if necessary.
- Seal, leave to cool, and store in the fridge.
- Keep in a cool, dark cupboard for 3-5 days before opening, to allow the flavors to develop.

Keeps for up to 6 months unopened. Once opened, keep refrigerated and eat within 4 weeks.

sweet pickled apricots

Once a year, in the summer, you can find the most adorable miniature apricots to pickle. I've even seen them in my corner store in Hackney. Served with yogurt they make the perfect instant dessert for an unexpected guest.

25–30 miniature apricots
⅔ cup white balsamic vinegar
⅔ cup white wine vinegar
⅓ cup water
1 cup granulated sugar
2 tbsp honey
a pinch of sea salt
1 star anise
½ cinnamon stick
1 lemon, zest and juice
¼ tsp pink peppercorns

makes
2 x 17-ounce or 1-liter jar

season summer

how to eat
these sweet little treats are delicious with lightly spiced yogurt or ice cream with toasted pistachios or almond slivers

- With a needle, prick the mini apricots 3 or 4 times to allow the sweet vinegar brine to penetrate them.
- Put all of the ingredients, apart from the apricots, into a medium, stainless steel saucepan, and simmer gently, dissolving the sugar and infusing the spices for about 5 minutes. Remove from the heat and leave to cool.
- Put the apricots into warm, dry sterilized jars, pour in the spiced brine to fill the jars to about ¼ inch below the rim and seal.
- Store sealed for at least 4 weeks in a cool, dark place, allowing the flavors to permeate the fruit before eating.

Keeps unopened for up to a year. Once opened, keep refrigerated and eat within 4 weeks.

roasted pineapple and coconut sweet pickle

Sweet pickles have a deliciously tart flavor and make a wonderfully simple, healthy pudding served with spiced yogurt. You can also serve them with cream or ice cream for a more indulgent treat. This one is both sweet and spicy, a combination I particularly love.

½ pineapple
1 tsp chili flakes
2 tsp raw sugar
¼ cup coconut flakes
¾ cup rice wine vinegar
½ cup water
⅔ cup superfine granulated sugar
1 cinnamon stick, broken into
    quarters
¼ tsp sea salt
¼ tsp black peppercorns

makes
4 x 8-ounce jars or 1-liter jar

season summer

how to eat
with coconut ice cream or Greek yogurt spiced with ground cinnamon

- Preheat the oven to 350°F.
- Slice off the skin from the pineapple. Cut the flesh into ⅓ inch bite-size cubes.
- Toss the pineapple in a roasting pan with the chili flakes and raw sugar and bake for 15 minutes.
- Mix in the coconut flakes and bake for another 5 minutes. Remove from the oven and leave to cool.
- Put the remaining ingredients in a medium, stainless steel pan and warm slowly at a gentle simmer, stirring to dissolve the sugar and infuse the spices, for about 5 minutes. Remove from the heat and leave to cool.
- Fill the warm, dry sterilized jars with the chili-roasted pineapple and coconut, then pour in the brine until it is about ¼ inch below the rim. Gently tap out any air bubbles and seal tightly.
- Store in the fridge for 3–5 days, allowing the flavors to develop before eating.

Keeps unopened in the fridge for up to 4 months. Once opened, keep refrigerated and eat within 4 weeks.

blueberries in a pickle

Pickled fruits are just as delicious as pickled vegetables. Not all fruits work, but blueberries are quite comfortable in a vinegar brine. I particularly like these on top of toasted, seeded sourdough bread smothered with cottage or cream cheese and smoked mackerel.

1 cup cider vinegar
1 cup water
⅔ cup granulated sugar
1 tsp sea salt
3 tbsp fresh ginger
1 lime, zest only
1 lemon, zest only
8 whole cloves
4 black or pink peppercorns
2 green cardamom pods
1 cinnamon stick, halved or
  quartered
2 star anise
2 lbs blueberries

makes
4 x 8-ounce tall jars or 1-liter jar

season summer to early autumn

how to eat
try with goat cheese and watercress on seeded toast, or on top of smoked mackerel and crème fraîche canapés

The brine can be prepared and refrigerated the day before, but don't keep it for more than a week. When ready to pickle, gently heat it up and use warm.

- In a medium, stainless steel pan, combine the vinegar, water, sugar, and salt and simmer gently stirring to dissolve the sugar.
- Thinly slice the ginger, then add to the hot brine with the lime and lemon zests and all the spices. Leave to infuse off the heat for at least 10 minutes.
- Remove the spices from the brine with a slotted spoon and distribute them as evenly as you can between the warm, dry sterilized jars.
- Stack the blueberries in the jars then pour in the warm brine, filling to about $\frac{1}{4}$ inch below the rim. Gently tap out any air bubbles, add more brine if the level drops below $\frac{1}{4}$ inch, and seal.
- Rest in a cool, dark place for at least 48 hours (if you can) before eating.

Keeps unopened for up to a year. Once opened, refrigerate and eat within 4-6 weeks.

jams, jellies, and compotes

Making jams and jellies didn't come naturally to me, in the way chutney had, at the beginning of Newton & Pott. I had made jam before but only a small batch from redcurrants which are high in pectin; therefore it set easily. So, when it came to creating the larger batches required for Newton & Pott, it took me a while to understand the chemistry behind setting a jam or jelly.

Since then I have learned so much and I'm pleased to be able to pass on this knowledge. I have kept the batch sizes small and focused on achievable recipes, so hopefully you will find making jam much more rewarding than I did at the start.

jams and marmalades

With their sweet, bright warmth, jams are the essence of freeze-framing a season into a jar. The French are generally acknowledged as the masters of jam so when I started jam-making I went to Paris for a confiture reconnaissance. In France, the confitures are plentiful and the flavor variations are endless. This inspired me to play around with different combinations in my own jams, adding herbs, spices, flowers, and alcohols. I still have to convince some customers they aren't having a sneaky tipple with the alcohol-infused ones. The actual alcohol evaporates in the high temperatures leaving just the rich flavor of the spirit to resonate, but some people just can't get their heads around this.

jellies

Clear jellies make me so happy. They have to be one of the prettiest preserves you can make and I like to give as much thought to how they look as to how they taste. I play around with the crystal-clear bright colors, by floating flowers, chilis, or herbs in them to look like snowflakes or spiders lost in space.

You can create jellies out of almost any fruit and sometimes vegetables. In most cases, the fruit is boiled to release the juices and the natural pectin, then strained overnight through a muslin bag, leaving you with a delightful fruit-flavored, brightly colored clear liquid that becomes the basis of your jelly. By adding sugars, acid, and sometimes extra-natural pectin, you create a chemical reaction that then produces a firm jelly, solid enough to float herbs, spices, and even flowers in.

compotes

Compotes are not strictly preserves because you need to keep them in the fridge and eat them within a few days. But I've included them anyway because, with their rich fruit colors and flavors, they feel spiritually akin to jam. And what a treat they are with breakfast. Lower in sugar than jam, they are the best thing on porridge or yogurt.

key ingredients

Fruit, sugar, pectin, and acid—these are the four essentials when making jams and jellies.

Fruit: Different fruit has different levels of pectin and acidity, and these two things, along with the quantity of sugar and the temperature, will determine the set of your jam or jelly. Choose fruit that is fresh and in season, and unlike with chutney, fruit that is slightly under or only just ripe. The recipes in this section will guide you as to the pectin levels of individual fruits.

Sugar: This is what preserves your fruit and allows it to keep, alongside proper sterilization and sealing. Adding pectin can help you reach setting point without the jam tasting too sweet. There are high-set or low-set jams, depending on whether you want your jam firm or runny. The more sugar, the harder and sweeter the jam; less sugar gives a softer result, more like a compote.

Pectin: This is a natural gelling agent found in the flesh, seeds, skin, and stones of most fruit and a few vegetables. Some fruits have high pectin levels while others have lower levels and need the help of added pectin to set into jams or jellies. Powder or liquid, slow- and rapid-set pectin can be bought online. But I generally like to use sugars with added pectin as it is easier to get the levels right without over- or under-adding. There are exceptions to the rules and some jellies need a helping hand to achieve a hard set, so you do need to add pectin sometimes. I based the portions of these recipes on Ball's Real Fruit Classic Pectin.

Acid: This breaks down the fruit and releases the pectin, which is essential for jam and jelly setting. Most fruits contain natural acids which aid this process but I almost always use lemon juice in my jams and jellies too, not only to encourage this process but also to cut through the sweetness, giving the preserve a hint of sharpness.

key equipment

- A collection of glass jars of varying sizes, with matching lids.
- A large, heavy-bottomed stainless steel pan, preferably a jam or preserving pan that widens at the top. Copper pans can be used and are very pretty but I tend not to use them as the metal reacts with some high acidic fruits which can taint the taste of the preserve.
- Wooden spoons, with long handles, as hot preserves tend to spit.
- Large muslin squares and kitchen string or jelly bags, for drip-sieving jellies.
- Small muslin squares and kitchen string, to make bags for holding seeds and stones and sometimes spices.
- A funnel with a wide, short spout that fits into your jars.
- Oven mitts, for handling the warm sterilized equipment.
- A ladle or heatproof jug for pouring the jam into jars and a spatula for scraping out the remains.
- A blender, food processor, or a food mill for puréeing.
- A sugar/jam thermometer to measure the setting point of the jam.
- Small plates to go in the freezer for the wrinkle test (see method tips on next page).

method tips

- Rinse and dry the fruit, then de-stalk, peel, core, pit, and hull as necessary. Discard any bruised, brown, or rotting pieces. Chop the fruit into pieces, as per the recipe, but with berries, leave some whole to give you nice plump fruit on your toast.

- Clean and sterilize everything: pan, ladle, funnel, jug, jars, and lids (see page 13 for the method), and make sure your jars and lids are completely dry before filling. Your jams will keep longer if you are meticulous about this.

- With jams: You generally add the sugar after the fruit has softened on the heat and becomes mushy, unless you want a few whole berries/ fruit pieces in the mix. In this case keep a few back and add these after the sugar has dissolved.

- With marmalades: Wash and scrub citrus peel, especially if it is waxed, because you will be eating it. You need to blanch the peel first, to give it a softer texture, so it needs to be boiled in water for a while before you add the sugar.

- With jellies: Almost all jellies need to be sieved because you use only the fruit juice, not the pulp. You do this by putting the boiled fruit into a large piece of muslin, tied up with some kitchen string, or into a store-bought jelly bag, then placing the bag over a large bowl to catch the juice. Leave to strain overnight, or for at least 8 hours, resisting the urge to squeeze the fruit-filled bag and allowing it to drip at its own speed; squeezing it will make the liquid cloudy whereas leaving it to strain naturally will produce a lovely clear juice. Discard the leftover pulp or you can use it to make a healthy snack like Fruit Leathers (see page 218). Add the sugar after the juice has warmed up a bit but before it reaches a boil. Only bring the mixture to a boil once the sugar has completely dissolved.

- With compotes: As there is less sugar in a compote, they need to thicken, not set. They don't need storing in sterilized jars, just in the fridge, and they should be eaten within a few days.

- As mentioned, I portioned out the sugar–pectin amounts based on Ball's Real Fruit Classic Pectin. I would advise to use the pectin measurements as a guide and experiment with more or less pectin for the desired consistency of your jams and jellies. Adding more pectin will produce a harder set; using less yields a softer set.

- Wrinkle set test: Use this test to check whether your jams or jellies are ready to be put into jars. Place a few small plates in the freezer before starting to cook. When the jam or jelly reaches between 219°F

and 222°F on the thermometer, or starts to make larger popping
bubbles, rather than rolling foamy ones, take off the heat and test for
the setting point as follows. Take a plate from the freezer and drip a
little of the jam onto it. Put the plate in the fridge for a minute, then test
the mixture by pushing it with your finger. If it wrinkles gently, then it's
soft set and ready for jarring. If you would like a harder set, return the
mixture to the heat, continue to boil between 219°F and 222°F, then test
again as necessary until you reach the desired set. When the wrinkle
stays in place when you push the mixture, this is known as a hard jelly
set and it means your jam is ready. If you are adding any liquids, such as
alcohol, to your jam at the end, it's best to make a slightly harder set as
the liquid will soften the mix a fraction.

- Once the jam or jelly is ready, remove from the heat and skim off any
  scum that has formed with a slotted spoon. At this stage, stir in any
  alcohol, petals, essences, or herbs that you are using.

- Allow the jam to settle for 5 minutes before pouring into warm sterilized
  jars. However, if you are adding floating fruits, flowers, spices, or herbs,
  rest the mixture for 5–8 minutes in the pan so it starts the setting
  process slightly before jarring. With marmalade, for example, this will
  help distribute the peel evenly in the jar.

- Pour into jars leaving at least ⅛ inch space between the top of the jam
  and the rim and seal immediately with hot sterilized, twist-on lids. Use
  oven gloves to do this because everything will be very hot.

- Clean off any sticky residue from the outside of the jar with a warm wet cloth and allow the preserve to cool. When cool enough to handle, label the jars with the name of the jam and the date.

- When preserved, sterilized, and sealed properly following the above instructions, the jams should last for 6 months to a year. Once opened, store in the fridge and eat within the time specified for each recipe.

breaking the rules

There are lots of amazing fruit trees in the city as well as in the countryside so try foraging for berries, plums, flowers, and fruits. This is not really breaking the rules unless you trespass but it is fun to do and you end up with a medley of different goodies. Make sure you thoroughly wash and dry your gatherings to ensure they are free from environmental impurities.

possible problems

- If your jam is too runny, once jarred and cooled, this means it hasn't set properly and is lacking pectin. Re-boil with added liquid pectin or pectin powder, mixed with a little sugar, then do the wrinkle set test again and again until it reaches your desired set. Once ready, re-jar into warm, dry sterilized jars.
- If your jam is too hard, you have over-boiled it. This can't be corrected so be careful when doing the wrinkle set test next time. On the plus side, you can still eat the jam: serve it like a fruit cheese, such as Membrillo (see page 229).
- If your jam or jelly has crystalized after being open for a while in the fridge, the sugar has returned to its original crystal state. Place the sealed jar in a pan of cold water and slowly bring to a gentle simmer to melt the crystals. Carefully remove the jar from the pan, open it, add a squeeze of lemon juice, mix, then reseal.
- If you find mold in your jam or jelly when you open your jar for the first time, this means that bacteria has grown in the jar because it wasn't sterilized properly. It is important to follow the correct sterilization procedures (see page 13) if you want your preserves to last.

summer berry and lemon thyme jam

The arrival of summer is extremely exciting, not just because of the warm weather but because of the incredible wealth of red berries summer brings. Berries are a joy to eat and to cook with and this jam allows you to have lots of them in one hit. You can use whichever berries you want for this recipe, from some of the more common to the obscure like loganberries. Make sure you wash and gently dry them first, especially those which you may have foraged.

3⅓ lbs mixed strawberries, blackberries, raspberries
1⅓ tbsp water
¼ cup lemon juice (about 1 large lemon)
4 cups granulated sugar
6 tbsp classic pectin
2 tbsp fresh lemon thyme leaves

makes
6–7 x 8-ounce jars

season summer to early autumn

how to eat
this is the perfect breakfast jam, for granola, yogurt, toast, everything!

- If using strawberries in your mix, halve them, then put them with all the other berries in a large jam pan with the water and soften for 10 minutes on a moderate heat.
- Add the lemon juice, sugar, and pectin, stirring to dissolve the sugar, then bring it to boil at around 219°F, stirring intermittently, for another 20 minutes. Use the wrinkle test, as needed, to check when it has reached a soft setting point.
- When it is ready, take off the heat, skim off any scum from the surface and stir in the lemon thyme leaves.
- Leave to sit for 5 minutes, then ladle into warm, dry sterilized jars and seal.

Keeps unopened for up to 6 months. Once opened, refrigerate and eat within 4–6 weeks.

baked peach and vermouth jam

Because peaches are so naturally sweet, it has taken a lot of trial and error to make
a peach jam that doesn't taste like pure sugar. The game changers I discovered were baking
the peaches, then infusing them in vermouth; this brings out a delicious depth
of flavor in the fruit.

4 lbs peaches
⅓ cup vermouth, extra-dry or rosso
3 cups granulated sugar
4 tbsp classic pectin
**3 tbsp lemon juice (about ½ large
  lemon)**
4 star anise

makes
6–7 x 8-ounce jars

season summer to early autumn

how to eat
use instead of fruit in individual
crumbles or spread on the base
of a galette

If you have time, bake the peaches the day
before and soak them in vermouth overnight
to infuse thoroughly. If you don't have time,
infuse for 1–2 hours.

- Preheat the oven to 350°F.
- Halve the peaches, keeping the stones in,
  place face down in a large baking tray and
  bake for around 40 minutes.
- When done, remove from the oven, rest for
  about 5 minutes, then peel off the skins, discard
  the stones, and keep to one side. Cut each half
  into 6 pieces.
- Wrap the peach stones in a small piece of
  muslin and tie into a bag with kitchen string.
- Place the peach pieces in a bowl, stir in the
  vermouth, and leave to rest, covered, for
  1–24 hours.
- Preheat the oven to the lowest setting, then
  warm 2 cups of the sugar in the oven for around
  10 minutes. Meanwhile, mix the pectin in the
  remainder of the unheated sugar.
- Put the alcohol-infused peach pulp in a large
  jam pan with the lemon juice, star anise, all
  of the sugar, and the muslin bag and bring to
  a boil.
- Continue to boil steadily, stirring while it
  thickens, for about 10–15 minutes.
- Use the wrinkle test to check the setting
  point, then, when ready, take off the heat,
  skim off any scum from the surface, and
  remove the muslin bag.
- Leave to sit for 5 minutes to thicken, then
  ladle into warm, dry sterilized jars and seal.

Keeps for up to 6 months unopened. Once
opened, refrigerate and eat within 4 weeks.

blackberry and gin jam

I like to add alcohol to my jams, much like a mixologist might put jam in a cocktail, and blackberry and gin are a classic match. By adding the gin at the end to the hot jam, the spirit content of the alcohol burns off leaving just the juniper flavor of the gin, without the hangover.

3⅓ lbs blackberries
1 cup water
7 cups granulated sugar
6½ tbsp classic pectin
2¾ tbsp lemon juice (about ½ large lemon)
¾ cup gin

makes
8 x 8-ounce jars

season late summer to autumn

how to eat
make up a layered granola and yogurt bowl, or slather on a piece of wholegrain toast or an English muffin

By adding ⅓ of the berries later in the process, you get whole fruit in the jam, adding texture to the mix.

- Place ⅔ of the berries in a large jam pan with the water and slowly bring to boil, softening the fruits for around 10 minutes.
- Add the sugar, pectin, and lemon juice and bring to boil, stirring to dissolve the sugar, then add the remainder of the blackberries.
- Boil rapidly, stirring constantaly, for 15–20 minutes.
- Use the wrinkle test to check the setting point, then, when ready, take off the heat and skim off any scum from the surface.
- Stir in the gin and leave for a few minutes so that the alcohol burns off.
- Ladle into warm, dry sterilized jars and seal.

Keeps unopened for up to 6 months. Once opened, refrigerate and eat within 4 weeks.

pear and lavender jam

If you like floral accents in your food you will love this jam. These two delicate flavors work beautifully together.

4½ lbs pears
2½ tbsp ml lemon juice (about
    ½ large lemon)
3½ cups granulated sugar
5 tbsp classic pectin
1 vanilla pod
1 tbsp edible dried lavender

makes
5–6 x 8-ounce jars

season spring, summer, autumn, winter

how to eat
on toasted English muffins, crumpets, or sourdough toast

- Peel and core the pears. Cut half of the pears into ¼ inch pieces and blend the other half in a food processor.
- Put the diced pears together with the blended pulp into a large jam pan with the lemon juice, 3 cups of the sugar, and the pectin.
- Bring slowly to boil on a moderate heat, stirring intermittently.
- Split the vanilla pod lengthwise, remove the seeds, then stir the seeds through the remaining sugar with a fork, mixing thoroughly. Add the vanilla sugar and vanilla pod to the pan and stir to dissolve.
- Boil steadily on a moderate heat for about 30 minutes, stirring intermittently, until it thickens and starts spitting.
- Use the wrinkle test to check for a soft setting point, then, when ready, take off the heat, remove the vanilla pod and skim off any scum from the surface.
- Stir through the dried lavender, then pour into warm, dry sterilized jars and seal.

Keeps unopened for up to 6 months. Once opened, refrigerate and eat within 4–6 weeks.

strawberry and pimm's jam

4½ lbs strawberries
3 tbsp water
⅓ cup lemon juice (about 1½ lemons)
4½ cups granulated sugar
½ cup classic pectin
⅔ cup Pimm's

makes
7–8 x 8-ounce jars

season summer

how to eat
amazing poured over vanilla
ice cream as an instant dessert.
Or, when making ice cream,
try folding it through the custard
for a strawberry ripple effect

This is a soft-set recipe so when you do the wrinkle test, make sure it's on the softer side.

- Halve the strawberries, place in a large jam pan with the water, and soften for 10–15 minutes on a moderate heat.
- Add the lemon juice, sugar, and pectin, stirring to dissolve the sugar while bringing the mixture to boil. Continue to boil steadily at around 219°F, stirring intermittently, for another 20–25 minutes.
- Use the wrinkle test to check the setting point, then, when ready, take off the heat and skim off any scum from the surface.
- While hot, stir in the Pimm's and leave for a few minutes so that the alcohol burns off.
- Ladle into warm, dry sterilized jars and seal.

Keeps for up to 6 months unopened. Once opened, refrigerate and consume within 4 weeks.

fig and lemon verbena tea jam

Picking fresh figs in Italy straight off the tree one summer is one of my favorite memories. They are so sweet it is like eating sunshine. I've only recently discovered the herb verbena; I really don't know where I have been! Its lovely lemony flavor is a perfect match with a variety of different fruits and it really complements figs.

½ cup lemon verbena tea leaves
½ cup boiling water
4½ lbs fresh figs
1 lbs lemon, zest and juice
2 cups granulated sugar

makes
4–5 x 8-ounce jars

season summer

how to eat
with sourdough toast and freshly brewed coffee in the morning, or on crostinis with ricotta and fresh figs at a dinner party

If you can't get your hands on lemon verbena tea leaves, try using the fresh herb leaves torn into pieces and added to the measure of water, or substitute it with some brewed green tea.

- Steep the verbena tea leaves in boiling water for 5 minutes, then strain and set the liquid aside.
- Remove the skins of the figs by cutting off the tops and bottoms, then peeling the skin back. Cut each fruit into 8 pieces.
- Put all the ingredients (including the verbena-steeped water) in a large jam pan and bring to a boil.
- Continue to boil on a moderate heat, stirring frequently for around 15–20 minutes until the mixture thickens into a jammy consistency. It will thicken rather than reach a setting point so bear this in mind when determining the desired consistency.
- When ready, take off the heat, remove any scum, and leave to sit for 5 minutes, then ladle into warm, dry sterilized jars and seal.

Keeps for up to 6 months unopened. Once opened, refrigerate and consume within 4 weeks.

apricot and amaretto jam

Amaretto, with its unique flavor of fermented almond, tastes great in apricot jam. This makes sense because amaretto (derived from *amaro*, Italian for bitter) is traditionally made from apricot kernels. These days apricot kernels are used interchangeably with almonds as the basis for the spirit, which is testament to the perfect flavor match between almond and apricot.

5 cups granulated sugar
3 lbs firm, ripe apricots
1 lemon, juice, peel and pips
¾ cup water
½ cup amaretto

makes
6 x 8-ounce jars

season summer

how to eat
smother on a warm croissant
with butter, or drizzle over granola
and yogurt

- Preheat the oven to 230°F. Place the sugar in a baking tray in the oven to warm through for about 10 minutes.
- Cut the apricots into 8 pieces each, removing the kernels but keeping them for use later.
- Peel the lemon, using a knife, then juice the fruit, keeping the seeds.
- Place the apricot kernels, lemon seeds, and peel into a square of muslin and tie into a bag with kitchen string.
- Put the apricots with the water, lemon juice, and muslin bag in a large jam pan over a moderate heat, and cook for about 10 minutes until softened and thick.
- Reduce the heat, add the warmed sugar, and stir for 5 minutes until the sugar has dissolved.
- Increase the heat and boil rapidly for around 20 minutes. The jam will rise up in the pan so stir it constantly to keep the heat evenly distributed and prevent it from sticking and burning.
- Use the wrinkle test to check the setting point, then, when ready, take off the heat and skim off any scum from the surface. Remove the muslin bag.
- While hot, stir in the amaretto and leave for a few minutes so that the alcohol burns off.
- Ladle into warm, dry sterilized jars and seal.

Keeps for up to 6 months unopened. Once opened, refrigerate and eat within 4 weeks.

vanilla peach jam

Peaches epitomize summer for me so it is a must to preserve them when they are in season. This sweet and delicious jam is like summer in a jar.

3 lbs peaches
1 vanilla pod
2½ cups granulated sugar
4 tbsp classic pectin
4 tbsp lemon juice (about 1 lemon)

makes
4–5 x 8-ounce jars

season late summer to early autumn

how to eat
use to sandwich shortbread together
to make a really peachy jam cookie

The peaches need peeling for this recipe. Do this by cutting a cross on their base, blanching them in boiling water for a couple of minutes, then dunking them in ice-cold water. The skins will peel off very easily.

- Peel, halve, and pit the peaches, then chop into ½-inch pieces. Put the fruit into a large jam pan.
- Split the vanilla pod lengthwise, remove the seeds, then add the seeds and pod to the peaches with the sugar, pectin, and lemon juice.
- Bring the mixture to boil, stirring often, and continue to boil for up to 1½ hours or until the jam thickens.
- Use the wrinkle test after 1 hour to check the setting point, then, when ready, take off the heat, remove the vanilla pod and skim off any scum from the surface.
- Ladle into warm, dry sterilized jars and seal.

Keeps unopened for up to 6 months. Once opened, refrigerate and eat within 4–6 weeks.

raspberry and rose jam

The floral edge makes this jam special. If the scent of roses isn't your thing you can experiment with other essences. I love the texture and look of the raspberry seeds in this jam, but if you prefer your jam smooth and seedless see the tip below.

2 lbs raspberries
3 tbsp water
4 tbsp lemon juice (about 1 lemon)
3½ cups granulated sugar
5 tbsp classic pectin
1½ tsp rose extract
1 tbsp edible dried rose petals

makes
5 x 8-ounce jars

season late summer to early autumn

how to eat
layer between sponge cake and whipped cream for a special occasion Victoria sponge cake. Or try on English muffins or miniature homemade scones

For a seedless version, soften the raspberries, as per the recipe below, then firmly work the pulp through a fine sieve with a wooden spoon until only the seeds are left. Then mix just the liquid with ⅓ cup less of the sugar before bringing it to boil.

- Put the raspberries in a large jam pan with the water and lemon juice. Soften on a moderate heat for about 5 minutes.
- Mix in the sugar and pectin and bring to boil, stirring to dissolve the sugar.
- Continue to boil at a steady 219°F, stirring constantly, for 10–15 minutes.
- Use the wrinkle test to check the setting point then, when ready, take off the heat and skim off any scum from the surface.
- Leave to sit for 5 minutes then stir in the rose extract and petals.
- Ladle into warm, dry sterilized jars and seal.

Keeps unopened for up to 6 months. Once opened, keep in the fridge and eat within 4 weeks.

gooseberry and fennel seed jam

A former assistant, Sarah, loved this jam so much that she would eat all of the samples on my market stall. She decided that maybe she was craving the fennel taste so she bought a packet of fennel seeds to try to curb her jam consumption. As you can imagine, it wasn't the fennel that was so addictive . . .

3 lbs gooseberries
1¾ cups water
6¾ cups granulated sugar
2 tsp fennel seeds

makes
7–8 x 8-ounce jars

season late spring to early summer

how to eat
on toast, with cheese, or with both

Gooseberries are high in pectin and acid so there is no need to add lemon juice or pectin to this. The jam will change to a dark pinkish color when boiled long enough with the sugar, so don't be alarmed.

- Trim the ends of the gooseberries and place in a large jam pan with the water, then simmer gently until they start popping, bursting from their skins and softening to a pulp.
- Add the sugar, stir through until it dissolves, and bring to a boil.
- Continue to boil on a moderate heat for 30–40 minutes, stirring intermittently, and use the wrinkle test to check every so often until it reaches its setting point.
- Remove from the heat and skim off any scum from the surface.
- Stir through the fennel seeds then ladle into warm, dry sterilized jars and seal.

Keeps unopened for up to 6 months. Once opened, refrigerate and eat within 4–6 weeks.

blueberry, rhubarb, and lemon thyme jam

I'm a big fan of adding herbs and spices to jams. By combining different flavors, you are not simply making a spread for toast but creating something more versatile that can be used in unexpected ways.

1 ½ lbs rhubarb (fresh or frozen)
½ cup water
1 ½ lbs blueberries (fresh or frozen)
4 tbsp lemon juice (about 1 lemon)
3 ¾ cups granulated sugar
2 tsp fresh lemon thyme leaves
a pinch of sea salt

makes
6–7 x 8-ounce jars

how to eat
on top of thumbprint shortbread cookies, gently fold in while making ice cream for a ripple effect, or use instead of raspberry jam in a Bakewell tart

If you are using fresh rhubarb, cut it into ½-inch pieces; if it's frozen, defrost it first and add 3 tbsp less water. You can vary this recipe by using lemon basil or lemon verbena instead of the thyme.

- Soften the prepared rhubarb in a large jam pan with the water on a moderate heat for about 10 minutes. Add the berries, lemon juice, and sugar, then slowly bring to boil, stirring to dissolve the sugar.
- Continue to boil on a moderate heat for 20 minutes, stirring intermittently, until the liquid has reduced and the mixture has thickened to a jammy consistency.
- Use the wrinkle test to check for a soft setting point, then, when ready, remove from the heat.
- Skim off any scum from the surface, stir in the lemon thyme and salt then leave to sit for 5 minutes to infuse.
- Ladle into warm, dry sterilized jars and seal.

Keeps unopened for up to 6 months. Once opened, refrigerate and eat within 4 weeks.

pineapple and cracked pepper jam

Pineapple makes a surprisingly delicious marriage with cracked pepper. Its very sweet, tart taste is offset perfectly by the heat of the peppercorn. I use black peppercorns for this recipe but try pink or white for variation.

**5 lbs fresh pineapple (about
  2 pineapples)**
3⅓ tbsp lemon juice (about 1 lemon)
3½ cups granulated sugar
1 cup water
1 tbsp freshly ground black pepper

**makes
6–7 x 8-ounce jars**

how to eat
this is lovely with vanilla ice cream: the pineapple's sweetness pairs with the vanilla, while the hot pepper contrasts with the cold ice cream

Cutting up a pineapple is easier than it looks! First, trim off the ends, then, using a sharp knife, carefully slice off the skin, then remove the hard core at the base. Finally, slice it into discs or long strips, whichever you prefer.

- Chop the pineapple flesh into bite-size pieces.
- Blend 2 pounds pineapple flesh in a food processor or blender until smooth, then combine with everything else in a large jam pan. Bring slowly to boil, stirring to dissolve the sugar. This has a tendency to boil over so keep an eye on it.
- Continue to boil on a moderate heat for up to 40 minutes, stirring frequently while it thickens to prevent it sticking and burning.
- After 20 minutes, use the wrinkle test to check the setting point, then, when ready, take off the heat and skim off any scum from the surface.
- Stir in the freshly cracked black pepper, then ladle into warm, dry sterilized jars and seal.

Keeps unopened for up to 6 months. Once opened, refrigerate and eat within 4 weeks.

fig and orange jam

Figgy, boozy, orangey.

3 lbs fresh figs
3 large oranges
4 tbsp lemon juice (about 1 lemon)
⅓ cup Triple Sec, Grand Marnier,
**   or Campari**
4 cups granulated sugar

makes
6–7 x 8-ounce jars

season summer

how to eat
dollop on top of your morning
pancakes, or also great on crostinis
with ricotta and basil

This recipe requires 8 hours of macerating,
so plan for this when making it.

- Remove the skins of the figs by cutting off the tops and bottoms, then peeling the skin back. Cut each fruit into 8 pieces.
- Zest the oranges and set the zest aside. Peel them, discarding the peel and removing any white pith from the fruit, then cut each segment into 3 or 4 pieces.
- Combine the orange zest and flesh with the figs, lemon juice, alcohol, and sugar in a large glass bowl, stir thoroughly, cover, and leave for 8 hours or overnight.
- The next day, place the mixture in a large jam pan and slowly bring to boil, stirring to dissolve the sugar.
- Boil steadily at 219°F, stirring all the time so it doesn't stick to the bottom of the pan and skimming off any scum, for around 15–20 minutes.
- Use the wrinkle test to check the setting point, then, when ready, take off the heat and skim off any remaining scum from the surface.
- Ladle into warm, dry sterilized jars and seal.

Keeps unopened for up to 6 months. Once
opened, refrigerate and eat within 4–6 weeks.

two-tone peach and blackberry jam

This recipe is a bit of fun: two jams for the price of one. It looks amazing and gets a lot of attention on the Newton & Pott market stall. You could actually do this with most of the recipes that have a medium set as they will happily sit on top of each other without mixing together. Try Pear Jam (see page 137) without its added lavender with the Raspberry and Rose Jam (see page 145) on top.

peach jam
2 lbs peaches
2 cups granulated sugar
3 tbsp classic pectin
2½ tbsp lemon juice (about ½ lemon)

blackberry jam
3½ lbs blackberries
¾ cups water
4¼ cups granulated sugar
6¼ tbsp classic pectin
2 tbsp lemon juice (about ½ lemon)

makes
6–8 x 8-ounce jars

season late summer to early autumn

how to eat
with toast, and use a long-handled spoon to get the jams out of the jar, to make sure you get the best of both flavors!

The peaches need peeling for this recipe. Do this by cutting a cross on their base, blanching them in boiling water for a couple of minutes, then dunking them in ice-cold water. The skins will peel off easily. Make sure you start the peach jam first as it takes longer and, while it's cooking, prepare the blackberry jam. That way the jars won't cool too much before you pour in the second jam.

- Peel, pit, and dice the peaches. Combine all the peach jam ingredients together in a large jam pan and boil, stirring often, for 30–40 minutes.
- Use the wrinkle test to check the setting point, then, when ready, take off the heat and skim off any scum from the surface.
- Meanwhile, place the blackberries in a separate large jam pan with the water and slowly soften on a moderate heat for about 10 minutes.
- Add the sugar, pectin, and lemon juice, stir to dissolve, then bring to boil for about 15–20 minutes, stirring intermittently.
- Use the wrinkle test to check the setting point, then, when ready, take off the heat and skim off any scum from the surface.
- Mark a halfway line on the warm, dry sterilized jars and pour in the blackberry jam to fill up to this line. Let it sit for 5 minutes while it forms a seal and you finish the other jam.
- Once the peach jam is ready, pour it on top of the blackberry jam to fill the jars almost to the rim, and seal.

Keeps unopened for up to 6 months. Once opened, refrigerate and eat within 4–6 weeks.

rhubarb and strawberry jam

Rhubarb makes an appearance again! It's a great tart flavor for jams, especially when mixed with other berries such as strawberries and blueberries. If you can find them, try some of the more obscure summer berries in your mix like loganberries or boysenberries.

2 lbs rhubarb (fresh or frozen)
1 lb strawberries (or a mix of berries)
2⅓ cups granulated sugar
½ cup water
4 tbsp lemon juice (about 1 lemon)

makes
8–10 x 8-ounce jars

how to eat
stir through whipped cream for an instant fruit fool, and try topping it with homemade honeycomb to add some texture

If you are using fresh rhubarb, cut it into ½-inch pieces; if it's frozen, defrost it first and add 3⅓ tbsp less water. And keep some strawberries whole if you like, and add these when you return the pulp to the pan; this will give you nice chunks of fruit in your jam.

- Prepare the rhubarb as above and quarter the strawberries. Put both in a large jam pan with the sugar and water on a moderate heat and simmer for around 15 minutes, letting the juices release.
- Once the juice starts to cover the fruit, take off the heat and use a fine-mesh sieve to separate the pulp from the juice, reserving the pulp for later.
- In the same large pan, bring the juice to boil on a moderately high heat for about 20 minutes, to reduce it by half.
- Stir in the reserved fruit pulp and the lemon juice, then bring back to boil and boil steadily, stirring intermittently, for another 20–25 minutes.
- Use the wrinkle test to check the setting point then, when ready, take off the heat and skim off any scum from the surface.
- Ladle into warm, dry sterilized jars and seal.

Keeps unopened for up to 6 months. Once opened, refrigerate and eat within 4–6 weeks.

rhubarb and blood orange jam

There are two rhubarb seasons—the forced in late winter, then the maincrop from spring through to early summer—so I use it a lot at Newton & Pott. If you run out of time to make jam while it is in season, rhubarb can easily be frozen and used at a later date. Blood oranges also arrive in the US in the same cold months as forced rhubarb, so this is the perfect recipe to make to combat the winter bleakness. If you can't find blood oranges, just use ordinary ones.

6½ lbs rhubarb (fresh or frozen)
4 large blood oranges, zest and juice
1¼ cups water
4½ cups granulated sugar
6 tbsp classic pectin

makes
9–10 x 8-ounce jars

season for blood oranges
late autumn to winter

season for rhubarb
(forced) late winter
(maincrop) spring to early summer

how to eat
try using in a bread-and-butter pudding

If you are using fresh rhubarb, cut it into ½-inch pieces; if it's frozen, defrost it first and add 3⅓ tbsp less water.

- Put the prepared rhubarb, orange zest and juice in a large jam pan with the water and soften on a moderate heat for around 15 minutes.
- Add the sugar and pectin, stir to dissolve, and bring to boil, stirring intermittently, for up to 45 minutes.
- Rhubarb thickens rather than sets in this jam, unlike other jams, so use the trail test (see page 17) to decide when it's ready. For a soft set, check it from 30 minutes onward or, if you want a jammier consistency, cook it a little longer and check again.
- When you get the desired thickness, take off the heat and skim off any scum from the surface.
- Ladle into warm, dry sterilized jars and seal. Keeps unopened for up to 6 months. Once opened, refrigerate and eat within 4 weeks.

pluot and almond jam

This is a sweeter jam equivalent of my Plum and Almond Chutney (see page 50) using pluots, a hybrid of a plum and an apricot, instead. I often cross-pollinate my jam and chutney flavor ideas because it feels right that similar techniques should feed into each other. And, since I love to get some texture in my jam, the almond adds a pleasing, slight crunch.

5 cups granulated sugar
3⅓ lbs ripe pluots
1¼ cups water
⅓ cup lemon juice (about 2 lemons)
⅓ cup slivered almonds

makes
7–8 x 8-ounce jars

season summer

how to eat
on toast, scones, English muffins, and crumpets

- Preheat the oven to 230°F. Place the sugar in a baking tray and warm through in the oven for about 10 minutes.
- Halve the pluots and remove their stones then cut each half again so that you have quarters.
- Put the pluots, water, and lemon juice in a large jam pan, bring to boil on a moderately high heat, and simmer for around 15–20 minutes, until the fruit is soft.
- Stir in the warmed sugar, then lower the heat and simmer gently, stirring until the sugar has dissolved.
- Add the slivered almonds and bring back to a boil, stirring and cooking for another 15–20 minutes.
- Use the wrinkle test to check for the setting point then, when ready, take off the heat and skim off any scum from the surface.
- Ladle into warm, dry sterilized jars and seal.

Keeps unopened for up to 6 months. Once opened, refrigerate and eat within 4–6 weeks.

chocolate and raspberry jam

Ok, this isn't really a jam; it is more like a raspberry chocolate spread. It is rich and decadent and a pure delight to spread on toast.

2 lbs raspberries
4¼ cups granulated sugar
4 tbsp lemon juice (about 1 lemon)
½ lb bitter chocolate, at least 70% cocoa solids

makes
3–4 x 8-ounce jars

season summer to autumn

how to eat
with sourdough toast and butter, or use as the filling for a sweet brioche

This recipe needs to stand overnight, so some time and patience is required, but it's absolutely worth it.

- Put the raspberries into a large saucepan with the sugar. Stir on a moderate heat until the sugar has dissolved.
- Remove from the heat and use a spatula to push the berries through a fine-mesh sieve to separate the seeds from the pulp.
- Discard the seeds, return the pulp to the saucepan, and stir in the lemon juice.
- Slowly warm the mixture on a low heat, keeping it just below a boil. Break the chocolate up into pieces, then add to the pan, stirring while letting them melt gradually.
- Once the chocolate has melted, take off the heat. The mixture may separate, so cover and leave to cool overnight to allow it to settle and smooth out.
- The next day, bring the mixture to a hard rolling boil for 5 minutes in a saucepan, stirring constantly.
- Use the wrinkle test to check for a firm set and, when ready, take off the heat.
- Ladle into warm, dry sterilized jars and seal.

Keeps unopened for up to 8–10 months. Once opened, refrigerate and eat within 4–8 weeks.

rhubarb and pear jam

With its dull tan brown color (use pink-forced rhubarb for a slightly rogue variation), this jam is not as pleasing to the eye as others but what it lacks in looks it makes up for in taste: delicate, tart, and absolutely delicious.

2 lbs rhubarb (fresh or frozen)
2 lbs pears
$\frac{1}{3}$ cup water
2 lemons, zest and 50ml of juice
2 cups granulated sugar
$3\frac{1}{2}$ tbsp classic pectin

makes
7–8 x 8-ounce jars

season spring, summer, autumn, winter

how to eat
as a healthy dessert with Greek yogurt, or as a naughty dessert as a crumble base

If you are using fresh rhubarb, wash and cut into $\frac{1}{2}$-inch pieces; if it's frozen, defrost it first and add $3\frac{1}{3}$ tbsp less water.

- Prepare the rhubarb as above and peel, core, and chop the pears into bite-size cubes.
- Place the rhubarb and pears with the water in a large jam pan and soften on a moderate heat for around 15 minutes.
- Add the lemon zest, lemon juice, sugar, and pectin to the pan and slowly bring to a boil, stirring to dissolve the sugar.
- Boil rapidly at around 219°F for up to 45 minutes, stirring intermittently. Be careful as the rhubarb will start to bubble and spit as you stir.
- Since the rhubarb thickens rather than sets like other jams, use the trail test (see page 17) to decide when it's ready. For a soft set, check it after 30 minutes onwards or, if you want a jammier consistency, cook it a little longer and check again.
- When it's ready, take off the heat, skim off any scum, ladle into warm, dry sterilized jars and seal.

Keeps unopened for up to 6 months. Once opened, refrigerate and eat within 4–6 weeks.

caramel apple and rum jam

If you want to make jam in-between seasons, one reliable year-round staple is the apple. This is a perfect recipe to turn to in the winter when there is little else on offer in your corner store. As this jam is mixed with a little tipple of rum, you have another warming reason to treat yourself in the chillier months.

3 cups granulated sugar
1 cup water
3 tbsp lemon juice (about ½ large
  lemon)
1 vanilla pod
a pinch of sea salt
5 cups unsweetened apple sauce
3½ tbsp dark rum

makes
5–7 x 8-ounce jars

how to eat
for breakfast on toast, yogurt, porridge, or bircher muesli

If you don't have apple sauce on hand, make some by peeling, coring, and slicing about 5–6 apples, putting them in a lidded pan with ⅓ cup of water, then cooking, covered, until soft, around 20 minutes. Blend until smooth. Or make ahead of time and freeze it for another day. Make sure you defrost it thoroughly before starting the recipe.

- Spread 2 cups of the sugar evenly across the base of a large jam pan. Mix the water with the lemon juice, then carefully pour over the sugar. This mixture needs to be as level as possible to ensure the sugar cooks evenly.
- Heat the mixture gently, without moving or stirring it, until it boils and turns a golden tawny brown. Watch the mixture carefully so that it doesn't turn too dark.
- While the sugar is caramelizing, split the vanilla pod lengthwise and mix the seeds and the pod with the remaining sugar and salt in a small bowl.
- When the caramel is ready, remove from the heat and stir in the apple sauce, the vanilla sugar, and vanilla pod. Be careful as it will spit.
- Return to the heat and gently warm, stirring until the sugar dissolves.
- Bring to boil and boil steadily at around 219°F for about 15–20 minutes. Stir steadily as it will spit as it thickens. The jam is ready when a wooden spoon leaves a clear trail on the bottom of the pan.
- When it is ready, take off the heat, remove the vanilla pod, and stir in the rum.
- Ladle into warm, dry sterilized jars and seal.

Keeps unopened for up to 6 months. Once opened, refrigerate and eat within 4–6 weeks.

damson plum and orange jam

If you are lucky enough to get your hands on some damson plums in their short summer season, grab as many as you can! If you don't use them all immediately they freeze extremely well. You can make so many delicious things with them: jams, jellies, fruit cheeses (see page 224), and boozy liqueurs (see page 261). Damsons are in fact bitter little plums and, since they contain lots of natural pectin, they make a handy companion in a preserver's kitchen. This recipe is versatile, so feel free to substitute whatever plums are in season near you.

8½ cups granulated sugar
2 lbs damson plums (fresh or frozen)
2¼ cups water
3 oranges, zest and juice

makes
6–7 x 8-ounce jars

season late summer

how to eat
spread a layer on the base of a Bakewell tart instead of raspberry jam. Plum jam is also a treat with cheese

- Preheat the oven to 230°F. Put the sugar in a baking tray, then warm through in the oven for about 10 minutes.
- Put the plums in a large, lidded heavy-bottomed pan with the water and slowly bring to boil. Lower the heat, cover and simmer gently for 45–50 minutes until the plums are soft and the stones start to come out.
- Add the orange juice and warmed sugar to the plums, stir through to dissolve the sugar, and bring to boil, then continue to boil on a moderate heat for around 15–20 minutes, stirring intermittently.
- Use the wrinkle test, as needed, to check if it has reached its setting point.
- When ready, take off the heat and skim off any scum or stones that have surfaced.
- Sieve the jam, or use a jam muddler, to remove any remaining stones or skins.
- Stir through the orange zest, then ladle into warm, dry sterilized jars and seal.

Keeps unopened for up to 6–8 months. Once opened, refrigerate and eat within 4–6 weeks.

grapefruit and chili marmalade

Grapefruit makes delicious marmalade. This is a great recipe and it's not difficult at all. The chili is a nice twist but you can have it without or be adventurous and substitute it with something else like ¾ cup of pomegranate juice, ¾ cup whisky, 8 torn basil leaves, or 4 tbsp of peeled and grated fresh ginger.

5 large pink or yellow grapefruit
2½ cups water
4¼ cups granulated sugar
2 tsp chili flakes

makes
5–6 x 8-ounce jars

season autumn to winter

how to eat
great with cheese, but try whisking it into a salad dressing, or add to a soy sauce marinade

- Quarter the grapefruit and remove the peel. Remove as much of the white pith from the peel of 3 of the grapefruit, then slice this peel into long thin slices. Discard the peel from the other 2 grapefruits. Chop the flesh of all of the grapefruit into ⅓-inch pieces, discarding any seeds and pith.
- Put the sliced peel in a saucepan, cover with the water, and bring to boil. Reduce the heat, cover and simmer for 10–15 minutes, then remove from the heat and set aside, still in the hot water.
- Put the grapefruit flesh and any juice it creates into a large jam pan with the boiled peel in hot water and 3¾ cups of the sugar. Bring to boil for 20 minutes at around 219°F, stirring intermittently.
- Add the remaining ½ cup of sugar to the pan with the chili flakes.
- Boil steadily, stirring constantly, for another 20 minutes.
- Use the wrinkle test to check if it has reached the desired setting point. If you are adding liquid instead of the chili flakes, make sure the set is on the firm side as adding liquid will soften it.
- When it is ready, take it off the heat and skim off any scum from the surface. Leave to sit for 5-8 minutes.
- Ladle into warm, dry sterilized jars and seal.

Keeps unopened for up to 6–8 months. Once opened, refrigerate and eat within 6 weeks.

orange and campari marmalade

This recipe celebrates the bitter palate by adding a splash of Campari to a traditional orange marmalade. It's like having a jam Negroni . . .

1 lb oranges
5 cups water
4 tbsp lemon juice (about 1 lemon)
3½ cups granulated sugar
3½ tbsp Campari

makes
4–5 x 8-ounce jars

season late winter

how to eat
add to a gin cocktail, or stir into a scone dough before baking

- Halve the oranges and juice them. Put the juice into a large jam pan.
- Scoop out all of the flesh and seeds from the juiced orange halves and discard. Scrape off as much of the white pith from the peel as possible and slice the peel as finely as you can with a sharp knife, preferably into ⅛-inch slices. Place in the pan with the orange juice and add the water and lemon juice.
- Bring to boil and simmer for 30–40 minutes until the peel is soft and loses its color a bit.
- Lower the heat and pour in the sugar, stirring until it dissolves.
- Once dissolved, bring back to a rapid boil at around 219°F, stirring continually for another 40–50 minutes.
- Use the wrinkle test to check when it has reached a firm setting point, then, when ready, take off the heat and skim off any scum from the surface.
- Stir through the Campari and stand for 5–8 minutes.
- Ladle into warm, dry sterilized jars and seal.

Keeps unopened for up to 6–8 months. Once opened, refrigerate and eat within 6 weeks.

meyer lemon marmalade

Meyer lemons have a flavor somewhere between a lemon and an orange. It's not a flavor for all palates but marmalade fanatics will love it.

2 lbs Meyer lemons
2 limes, zest and juice
4¼ cups water
3¾ cups granulated sugar

makes
4–5 x 8-ounce jars

season winter

how to eat
on whole-grain toast with a mackerel or salmon pâté

- Zest half of the Meyer lemons, then peel them, getting off as much pith as possible. Finally, chop the flesh into ½-inch cubes.
- Put the lemon zest and flesh in a large jam pan with the lime zest, lime juice, and water.
- Bring to boil for about 10 minutes, then reduce the heat and simmer for 20–40 minutes or until the peel has softened.
- Add the sugar, stirring until it has dissolved, then boil at around 219°F, stirring continually, for around 25–30 minutes.
- Use the wrinkle test to check when it has reached a firm setting point, then, when ready, take off the heat and skim off any scum from the surface. Leave to sit for 5–8 minutes.
- Ladle into warm, dry sterilized jars and seal.

Keeps unopened for up to 6–8 months. Once opened, refrigerate and eat within 6 weeks.

42 | COMMENT

blood orange marmalade

From their gothic color to their alluring taste, blood oranges are decadently gorgeous.
I try and use them in everything I can during their all-too-short season.

5½ lbs blood oranges
1 cup water
⅓ cup lemon juice (about 2 lemons)
3 cups granulated sugar

makes
4–5 x 8-ounce jars

season late autumn to early winter

how to eat
add to a vodka cocktail mix with a
dash of soda, or try folding into cake
dough before baking

- Cut 5 of the blood oranges into quarters, remove the flesh from the peel, and keep to one side. Scrape the pith from the quartered peels, then cut into ⅛-inch-thick slices. Peel the remainder of the blood oranges, this time discarding the peel, and remove as much pith as possible from the flesh. Chop the flesh (including the flesh of the first 5) into ½-inch pieces.
- Put the blood orange flesh into a large jam pan with the water and boil for about 10 minutes. Add the lemon juice and sugar and slowly bring back to boil, stirring to dissolve the sugar.
- Boil at around 219°F, stirring continually, for around 40–50 minutes.
- Use the wrinkle test to check if it has reached the desired setting point, then, when ready, take off the heat and skim off any scum from the surface.
- In a separate pan, cover the peel strips with boiling water and simmer for 4 minutes, strain, then stir through the marmalade mixture.
- Ladle into warm, dry sterilized jars and seal.

Keeps unopened for up to 6–8 months. Once opened, refrigerate and eat within 6 weeks.

orange and vanilla marmalade

Marmalade can be very bitter—this one has a slight bitterness from its peel—but the addition of vanilla seeds mellows this, giving it a smoother, milder flavor. This marmalade can even persuade a non-believer to love marmalade.

2 lbs oranges
1 lemon, zest and juice
6⅓ cups water
1 vanilla pod
7 cups granulated sugar

makes
8–9 x 8-ounce jars

season winter

how to eat
on warm, buttered, whole-grain toast or English muffins

- Cut the whole oranges in half, then slice into very thin semi-circles, about ⅛-inch thick. Discard any pips.
- Put the orange slices into a large jam pan with the lemon zest, lemon juice, and water, then boil on a high heat for 10 minutes.
- Reduce the heat to a simmer and cook for at least 40 minutes or until the peel has softened.
- Split the vanilla pod lengthwise and remove the seeds, stir the seeds through the sugar, then add the emptied pod and vanilla sugar to the pan, stirring until it dissolves. Boil at around 219°F, stirring continually, for around 25–30 minutes until it has darkened in color.
- Use the wrinkle test to check if it has reached the desired setting point and, when ready, take off the heat, remove the vanilla pod, and skim off any scum from the surface. Leave to sit for 5–8 minutes.
- Ladle into warm, dry sterilized jars and seal.

  Keeps unopened for up to 6–8 months. Once opened, refrigerate and eat within 6 weeks.

rhubarb and prosecco jelly

Decadent and delightful, this one is a special treat. Make for a birthday party, or freeze your pink forced rhubarb and make this just before Christmas for a bright pink translucent celebratory color.

2 lbs forced rhubarb (fresh or frozen), to make about 3 cups rhubarb juice
2 cups water
1 cup prosecco
2 cups granulated sugar
4½ tbsp classic pectin
¼ cup lemon juice (about 1 lemon)
a pinch of sea salt

makes
3–4 x 8-ounce jars

season late winter to early spring

how to eat
great in a Christmas trifle or a special birthday dessert, or just smother straight on toast

You need to start this recipe the day before you want to make the jelly. If you are using fresh rhubarb, cut it into ½-inch pieces; if it's frozen, defrost it first and add ¼ cup less water.

- Combine the prepared rhubarb and the water in a pan and bring to boil, then lower the heat to a simmer for about 30 minutes, or until the rhubarb has softened.
- Strain through muslin or a jelly bag overnight into a bowl (see page 126).
- The next day, measure the juice. For every 3 cups of rhubarb juice, add 1 cup of prosecco and $1^{3}/_{4}$ cups of sugar mixed with $4^{1}/_{2}$ teaspoons of classic pectin. Put the juice mixed with the prosecco, sugar, and pectin into a large jam pan, the larger the better as this recipe boils up quite high, and add the lemon juice and salt.
- Slowly bring to boil, stirring to dissolve the sugar, and boil for about 20–30 minutes at around 219°F, stirring often.
- Use the wrinkle test to check when it has reached a firm setting point, then, when ready, take off the heat and leave for 5 minutes to let any bubbles subside.
- Skim off any scum from the surface, ladle into warm, dry sterilized jars and seal.

Keeps unopened for up to 6–8 months. Once opened, refrigerate and eat within 6 weeks.

lime and saffron jelly

A lovely, sharp jelly with a dominant zesty lime flavor and pretty floating strands of aromatic saffron. They say saffron is worth its weight in gold so this is a jelly for kings—relax and claim your throne with some of this spread on toast.

12–14 limes
boiling water to cover
⅓ cup water
3½ cups granulated sugar
6 tbsp classic pectin
a pinch of saffron strands

makes
4–5 x 8-ounce jars

how to eat
great as a treat with cheese, or try serving it with baked white fish

You need to start this recipe the day before you want to make the jelly.

- Carefully peel 6 of the limes, scrape off as much white pith as you can from the peel then slice the peel into ⅛-inch-long thin strips. Set aside. Juice all of the limes (including the 6 peeled ones) and then chop them all into quarters, skins and all. Cover the limes (not the strips of peel) with boiling water, then soak for at least 2 hours.
- Strain through muslin or a jelly bag overnight into a bowl (see page 126).
- The next day, measure out 2 cups of the juice into a large jam pan, add the ⅓ cup of water and 3 cups of the sugar. Bring to a rapid boil on a high heat, stirring to dissolve the sugar.
- When dissolved, lower the heat and add the rest of the sugar mixed with the pectin. Boil at around 219°F for about 20 minutes, stirring often.
- Use the wrinkle test to check it has reached a firm setting point, then, when ready, take off the heat and leave for 5 minutes to let any bubbles subside.
- Skim off any scum from the surface, and stir through the reserved lime peel strips and the saffron.
- Ladle into warm, dry sterilized jars and seal.
- Turn the jars upside down then the right way up while setting so that the zest and saffron drift prettily through the jars.

Keeps unopened for up to 6–8 months. Once opened, refrigerate and eat within 6 weeks.

quince and cardamom jelly

Quinces are a very hard fruit that look similar to fat yellow pears. They can't be eaten raw; they must be cooked for a long time until their hard, white rawness transforms into a soft, delicate pink flesh that tastes quite delicious. I love it when quinces come into season as it reminds me that Christmas is on its way. This is the perfect accompaniment to festive roast duck or goose.

3½ lbs quinces (to make about 4 cups quince juice)
water to cover
4 cups granulated sugar to every 4 cups quince juice
2 tbsp lemon juice (about ½ lemon)
5 green cardamom pods

makes
5 x 8-ounce jars

season late autumn to mid-winter

how to eat
great with all cheeses but traditionally eaten with roast duck or goose as well

You need to start this recipe the day before you want to make the jelly. Quinces contain a lot of pectin so no added pectin is needed.

- Chop the whole quinces into 12 pieces each without coring or peeling. Put into a large pan with enough water to completely cover them. Bring to boil and simmer for at least 1 hour or until they are soft and can be mashed slightly.
- Strain through muslin or a jelly bag overnight into a bowl (see page 126).
- The next day, measure the quince juice into a large jam pan and add 3⅓ cups of sugar per 4 cups of juice. Add the lemon juice and cardamom pods.
- Slowly bring to boil, stirring to dissolve the sugar then boil at around 219°F for about 20 minutes, stirring often.
- Use the wrinkle test to check when it has reached a firm setting point then, when ready, take off the heat.
- Remove the cardamom pods and keep them to one side. Let the mixture sit for 5 minutes so that the bubbles settle.
- Rinse the cardamom pods under boiling water and pat dry. Place one in each warm, dry sterilized jar.
- Carefully skim off any scum from the surface then ladle into the jars and seal.

Keeps unopened for up to 6–8 months. Once opened, refrigerate and eat within 6 weeks.

cucumber and cracked pepper jelly

This recipe sounds like it shouldn't work—a vegetable made into a jelly? But it does and it's a must-try. I came up with it because one of my favorite things is sliced cucumber and cracked pepper on toasted dark rye bread with cream cheese. Now I simply use this spread.

3–4 large cucumbers (to make about 3½ cups cucumber juice)
4 cups granulated sugar to every 3 cups cucumber juice
1 cup white wine vinegar
7 tbsp classic pectin
1½ tsp freshly ground black pepper

makes
5–6 x 8-ounce jars

how to eat
use in a marinade with baked salmon, or float on top of a nutty soup

You need to start this recipe the day before you want to make the jelly. Place a few plates in the freezer as it may take a while to reach the point where you can do the wrinkle test.

- Grate the cucumbers whole, then blend in a food processor. Strain through muslin or a jelly bag overnight into a bowl (see page 126).
- The next day, measure the juice, then put it in a large jam pan. Stir in 4 cups of sugar for every 3 cups of cucumber juice, add the vinegar, and slowly bring to boil, stirring to dissolve the sugar.
- Simmer on a high heat for about 10 minutes. If and when the jelly rises to the top of the pan, lower the heat and stir to bring it down again.
- Mix together the remaining ½ cup of sugar with the pectin and add to the pan, dissolving the sugar then rapidly boiling at 219°F for 10–15 minutes, stirring often.
- Watch and stir the mixture continuously and be careful, as it will bubble and spit.
- Use the wrinkle test to check if it has reached a firm setting point. You may have to test a few times.
- When ready, take off the heat, skim off the scum from the surface, and stir in the freshly cracked black pepper. Leave to sit for 5 minutes.
- Ladle into warm, dry sterilized jars and seal.

Keeps unopened for up to 6–8 months. Once opened, refrigerate and eat within 6 weeks.

mango and lime jelly

**12 ripe mangoes (to make about
6⅓ cups mango juice)**
1 cup water
4 cups granulated sugar
3 tbsp classic pectin
1½ cups lime juice (about 10–12 limes)
3 limes, zest only

makes
5–6 x 8-ounce jars

how to eat
lovely with coconut ice cream
or in a tropical-themed trifle

You need to start this recipe the day before you want to make the jelly. For every 4 cups of mango juice, add 4 cups of sugar mixed with 3 tablespoons of pectin.

- Peel, halve, and pit the mangoes, then cut into cubes. Place with the water in a large pan and bring very slowly to boil, mashing the fruit to extract the juice.
- Simmer for around 15–20 minutes, then remove from the heat and strain overnight through muslin or a jelly bag into a bowl (see page 126). Keep the juice and discard the pulp (or make it into a Fruit Leather [see page 218]).
- Measure the strained mango juice and calculate the amount of sugar and pectin needed (as above). Put the juice and the sugar and pectin mix in a large jam pan with the lime juice and slowly bring to boil, stirring to dissolve the sugar.
- Once boiling, add the lime zest and continue to boil at 219°F for about 20–30 minutes, stirring often.
- Use the wrinkle test to check if it has reached a firm setting point then, when ready, take off the heat and leave to sit for 5 minutes, then skim off any scum from the surface.
- Ladle into warm, dry sterilized jars and seal.

Keeps unopened for up to 6–8 months. Once opened, refrigerate and eat within 6 weeks.

jalapeño and thai chili jelly

If you like it hot, this one's for you. It is also a great example of the versatility of jellies. Yes, this works with cheese, but it is also brilliant for pepping up simple dishes like white or oily fish or an understated bowl of Asian broth.

2 lbs apples
15 jalapeños
15 thai chilis
⅓ lb cranberries
6⅓ cups water

for every 3 cups of extracted juice
3 cups cider vinegar
4 cups granulated sugar
2 tbsp classic pectin

makes
5–6 x 8-ounce jars

how to eat
use in a marinade with baked salmon, and serve with bok choy and rice. Or add to miso soup for an added sweet kick

You need to start this recipe the day before you want to make the jelly. The amount of juice extracted in this recipe will determine the amount of vinegar, sugar, and pectin you will need. Calculate these according to the following: use equal measures of strained juice to vinegar (so if you have ½ cup of juice then add ½ cup of vinegar to it). Then, for every 3 cups of mixed juice and vinegar, add 2 cups of sugar mixed with 1 tablespoon of pectin.

- Roughly chop the apples, jalapeños, and 10 of the thai chilis and place them with the cranberries and water in a large pan. Bring to boil and simmer for at least 40–60 minutes.
- Once the fruit/chili mix has softened, mash lightly and strain through muslin or a jelly bag overnight into a bowl (see page 126).
- The next day, deseed and finely chop the remaining thai chilis.
- Measure the strained juice, calculate the measure of vinegar, sugar, and pectin needed (as above), combine in a large jam pan and bring to boil, stirring to dissolve the sugar.
- Once boiling, lower the heat and gently boil for around 30–40 minutes, stirring often.
- Use the wrinkle test to check when it has reached a firm setting point, then, when ready, take off the heat and skim off any scum from the surface.
- Stir through the chopped thai chilis, leave to sit for 5 minutes then ladle into warm, dry sterilized jars and seal.

Keeps unopened for up to 6–8 months. Once opened, refrigerate and eat within 6 weeks.

red currant and hibiscus jelly

The great thing about jelly preserves is they are perfect with cheese as well as spread on bread or toast. Hibiscus flowers look beautiful floating in this deep dark crimson jelly, but don't worry if you can't get your hands on them. Try hibiscus tea instead: the floral accents will still infuse the jelly with flavor.

6 dried hibiscus flowers
3⅓ cups boiling water
4½ lbs red currants (to make about
    4¾ cups redcurrant juice)
4¾ cups granulated sugar

makes
6 x 8-ounce jars

season summer

how to eat
with hard cheeses and on crostinis

You need to start this recipe the day before you want to make the jelly. Currants contain lots of pectin so there is a danger of overcooking this and the jelly setting too hard. Keep a close eye on the setting point by having several plates in the freezer so that you can do the wrinkle test a few times and catch the exact moment to take it off the heat and jar. You can use red or white currants for this recipe.

- Infuse the dried hibiscus flowers in the boiling water for 5 minutes, then take out the flowers, reserving them for later, and keep the infused water for cooking.
- Gently heat the currants with the infused water in a large pan for about 30–45 minutes, softening and mashing the fruit until it starts to break up.
- Strain the fruit through muslin or a jelly bag overnight into a bowl (see page 126).
- Measure 4¾ cups of the juice into a large jam pan and boil for 5 minutes.
- Stir in the sugar until it dissolves and bring back to boil for 5 more minutes.
- Reduce the heat and gently boil for around 10 minutes, stirring often.
- Use the wrinkle test to check the setting point, then, when ready, take off the heat, rest for 5 minutes, then skim off any scum from the surface.
- Place one hibiscus flower in each warm, dry sterilized jar, pour in the liquid jelly, and seal.
- Store each jar upside down for 10–15 minutes, then return right way up, so that the flower slowly rises during the setting of the jelly.

Keeps for 6–8 months unopened. Once opened, refrigerate and eat within 6 weeks.

blueberry and rose compote

Compotes have the consistency of jams but should be eaten within two to three days. They contain less sugar so are not technically preserved, so should be kept in the fridge. This is a small quantity so you'll find you eat it quickly anyway.

1 lb blueberries (fresh or frozen)
1½ cups granulated sugar
½ cup red wine or port (optional)
2 tsp edible dried rose petals
¼ cup lemon juice (about 1 lemon)

makes
2 x 8-ounce cups

season summer to early autumn

how to eat
for breakfast with porridge. Or, for a dessert, swirled onto rice pudding or into the base of a blueberry and rose crumble

If you can't get dried rose petals locally, try ordering them online. I find I use them a lot in my cooking, from baking to preserving. If you don't want to use red wine or port, substitute with ½ cup of water.

- Place the berries in a saucepan with all of the other ingredients on a moderate heat.
- Bring to a simmer and cook for around 15-20 minutes, mashing lightly and cooking until the liquid evaporates and reduces and the compote thickens to a jam-like consistency.
- Remove from the heat and serve immediately, or cool, then keep in the fridge covered and eat within 2-3 days.

cherry compote

Compotes are comforting in the cooler months but they deserve to be eaten in summer as well. What better way to celebrate the joys of summer than with fresh cherries. You just have to resist eating the fruit before they make it into the pan...

1½ lbs fresh cherries
½ cup raw sugar
¾ cup brandy
¾ cup orange juice

makes
1–2 x 8-ounce cups

season summer

how to eat
stir through whipped butter, mascarpone, or yogurt for an easy instant dessert. Try grating some dark chocolate and orange zest on top

Try warming this up just before serving.

- Pit the cherries, then put in a saucepan with all of the other ingredients. Bring to boil and simmer, stirring intermittently, until the cherries soften and start to release their juices, around 15–20 minutes, or until it has a jammy consistency.
- Remove from the heat and serve immediately, or cool, then keep in the fridge covered and eat within 2–3 days.

pear and blood orange compote

Compotes being low in sugar are a healthier alternative for a breakfast treat. Here, the sweetness of the pears balances out the tartness of oranges, and the blood oranges' vibrant color will perk up your mornings.

½ lbs blood oranges
1 lb pears
2 cups granulated sugar
½ tsp ground cinnamon

makes
2 x8-ounce cups

season winter

how to eat
have with your morning bircher muesli. Try in the base of homemade crème brûlée or panna cotta

- Zest two of the oranges, then peel and chop the flesh of all of them into ¼-inch pieces.
- Peel and core the pears, chopping the flesh into ½-inch cubes.
- Put the prepped oranges and pears in a saucepan on a moderate heat and cook for about 10 minutes, until they become soft and can be easily mashed.
- Add the sugar and cinnamon, then bring to a simmer and cook, stirring intermittently, for around 20–30 minutes until it has a jammy consistency.
- Remove from the heat and serve immediately, or cool, then keep in the fridge covered and eat within 2–3 days.

curds, candies, and fruit cheeses

This is the indulgent section of the book, the treats we allow ourselves between meals or after dinner. And because these sweet things are made from natural ingredients, making the most of the sugar and flavor inherent in fruits, you can eat them with a much clearer conscience than, say, a commercially produced chocolate bar. These recipes are guilt-free on another level too because making treats with seasonal produce has a lighter effect on the environment, just as handmade ones have a lighter effect on your processed food intake.

Here you will find out how to make creamy custard curds to dollop onto fresh buttered baguettes or to incorporate into your baking, how to create delectable, edible decorations for cakes and puddings and also how to make sweet yet healthy snacks. We all need to indulge from time to time, right?

curds

These should be eaten within a week or two of making. They contain eggs so are not strictly a preserve, but jarred up they look as attractive and tempting as any jam. Once you have tried making your own you won't buy one ever again. Store-bought curds are just not the same. For one thing, they have a suspiciously long shelf-life thanks to the addition of unedifying, stabilizing agents. Secondly, the commercial versions are a pale imitation of the incredible, delicious creaminess of homemade curd: a buttery, eggy sweetness cut through by the tartness of natural fruit juices or pulp. The contrast is truly dreamy.

candies

These sweet snacks are a great alternative to commercial sweets or chocolate. I have included them because we all need a little sugar sometimes. Here we learn to crystallize, dry-bake and sugar-coat fruit, flowers, and nuts.

fruit cheeses/fruit butters

Fruit cheeses are an old-fashioned preserve that deserve to be rediscovered. As with a lot of my recipes, I like to bring a modern approach to the tradition, by using new and interesting flavor combinations along with up-to-date tips and techniques. If you have ever tried the Spanish quince paste Membrillo (see page 229), then you have in fact already become acquainted with fruit cheese, perhaps without even realizing. They are firm-set preserves made from the pulp of fruit with added sugar, often set in molds. Traditionally served with hard cheese (the Spanish like their membrillo with Manchego), they are also delicious with cold meats, game, or simply as a midday snack with any old cheese on a cracker.

Fruit butters are similar to fruit cheeses but they have a softer, more spreadable set. They are great with cheese but also nice on their own smeared over a slice of bread. Fruit cheeses and butters take longer to make than jam as they must coagulate into a thick paste before setting in a mold or putting in a jar.

key ingredients

Fruit: Use just ripe, fresh fruit.

Sugar: Use white, raw, or granulated to crystallize candies and sweeten curds; sugar also plays an important part in the setting of fruit cheeses and butters.

Eggs, butter, nuts, spices, herbs, flowers: A few extras to make things more indulgent.

key equipment

- Collection of various different-size glass jars with lids, sterilized and completely dried for longer preservation (see page 13).
- Use a large heavy-bottomed stainless steel pan, preferably a large jam pan, for the fruit cheeses and butters.
- Wooden spoons: Constant stirring is required.
- Blender, food processor, or a food mill: for puréeing.
- Fine-mesh metal sieve: to pulp fruit for fruit cheeses or butters.
- Fine-mesh nylon sieve: for straining curds.
- Measuring jug and scales: to determine the ratios of pulp to sugar.
- Selection of different-shape molds, either individual ones or larger ones.
- Funnel, with a wide short spout, that fits into the top of the jars.
- Ladle and spatula: for putting the curds and cheeses in jars and scraping out the remains.
- Baking parchment and a large baking tray: for the dry-baking of candies and for crystallization.

method tips

- Rinse and dry the fruit, then de-stalk, peel, core, pit, and hull as necessary. Discard any bruised, brown, or rotting pieces. Chop the fruit into pieces, as per the recipe.
- Clean and sterilize everything: pan, ladle, funnel, jug, jars, and lids (see page 13 for the method), and make sure your jars and lids are completely dry before filling. Your preserves will keep longer if you are meticulous about this.

curds

- Curds take persistence to get right as various things can go wrong, notably the eggs scrambling, but cook them slowly, gently, and as long as it takes, as you would to make a custard, and there is no cause for mishap. The recipes in this chapter will walk you through it.
- If the curd scrambles, throw it away and start again.

candies

- These are all quite different, so read the recipe and follow the procedures step-by-step.

fruit cheeses/fruit butters

- You can use any fresh seasonal fruit. Simply rinse and dry, peel, and core or pit, as required, then roughly chop.
- Cover the fruit with cold water in a pan and bring to a simmer, then simmer until it has softened. Remove from the heat, then once slightly cooled, blend it in a food processor or with a food mill, then push through a fine-mesh sieve.
- The general ratio for fruit cheeses is: for every 2 cups of fruit pulp, add 1½–2 cups of granulated sugar, depending on the tartness of the fruit.
- Unlike jam, fruit cheeses are cooked in a pan on a moderate heat for up to 2 hours, and stirred frequently to dissolve the sugar. Once the mixture thickens and begins to hold a shape on a spoon, it is ready.
- If you are making a jelly, remember to save the leftover pulp that's been strained to make a fruit cheese—this way there is no waste and you get two products from the one fruit.
- Set in warm, dry sterilized jars and seal while still hot, or in lightly buttered/lined molds which are then slowly dry-baked in a very low heat for up to an hour.

breaking the rules

Try different fruits and don't be afraid to use vegetables that you think might work. Experiment with flavor combinations and mix up the fruits, herbs, or nuts.

passion fruit curd

One of the main reason curds work so well is the contrast of their comforting creamy texture with the sharp citrusy back notes. Passion fruit curds offer this same tart contradiction but with a more exotic feel. I never knew passion fruit were an exotic fruit until I got to the UK. We grew up eating them like the English might eat an apple.

12 passion fruits
4 medium eggs, plus 2 yolks
¾ cup superfine granulated sugar
⅓ cup unsalted butter

makes
2 x 6-ounce jars

how to eat
use to fill miniature tarts and put a raspberry on top, or fold into a cake mixture before baking it

- Remove the seeds of 9 passion fruits by scooping out the flesh, gently pulse-blending them, then pushing them through a fine-mesh sieve, discarding the seeds and keeping the juice. Cut the remaining 3 in half, scoop out the flesh, and set aside.
- Whisk the eggs, egg yolks, and sugar together until they are well mixed and light and frothy in texture.
- Gently melt the butter in a medium, heavy-bottomed pan on a low heat, then slowly stir in the eggs and sugar mix and the sieved passion fruit juice.
- Keep stirring and cooking over a low heat until the mixture has thickened to a custard-like consistency. This may take longer than you think, but be patient and don't be tempted to increase the heat as this may scramble the eggs.
- Remove from the heat and whisk in the remaining seeded passion fruit pulp.
- Ladle into warm, dry sterilized jars, filling them to about ¼-inch below the rim. Seal, leave to cool, then refrigerate.

Keeps for up to 1–2 weeks in the fridge.

citrus curds

I've called this citrus curd because I didn't want to limit it just to lemon. Limes or blood oranges also make delicious curds. Use the recipe as a template, but vary the fruits to make your own citrus burst.

3–6 lemons, limes, oranges, blood oranges—you need 1 cup juice, zest of half the fruit
4 medium eggs, plus 2 yolks
²⁄₃ cup superfine granulated sugar
½ cup (1 stick) unsalted butter

makes
2 x 6-ounce jars

how to eat
use in the middle of a Victoria sponge cake instead of jam, or in a citrus meringue pie

- Zest half of the fruit and juice as many of them as necessary to get 1 cup of juice. You may need more fruit, depending on their size/type. Sieve the juice, straining out any lumpy bits, and reserve.
- Whisk the eggs, egg yolks, and sugar together until they are well mixed and light and frothy in texture, then stir in the zest.
- Gently melt the butter on a low heat in a medium, heavy-bottomed pan. When completely melted, whisk in the citrus juice.
- Slowly pour in the egg mixture, stirring constantly.
- Continue stirring and cooking on the low heat until the mixture has thickened to a custard-like consistency. This may take up to 15 minutes but don't be tempted to increase the heat as this could scramble the eggs.
- Remove from the heat and whisk to remove any lumps.
- Ladle into warm, dry sterilized jars, filling them to about ¼ inch below the rim. Seal, leave to cool, and refrigerate.

Keeps for up to 1–2 weeks in the fridge.

berry curds

In the same way that the sour tartness of citrus marries well with sweet custardy curd, so does the slightly bitter tartness of most berries. Celebrate the berry season by making a bunch of different colored berry curds and give them to friends. You can have fun making up personalized labels and jars but make sure you tell them to keep their gifts in the fridge.

1 lb berries (e.g. blackberries,
   raspberries, loganberries,
   blueberries, cranberries)
¼ cup water
2 tbsp lemon juice
4 medium eggs, plus 2 egg yolks
1 cup superfine granulated sugar
½ cup (1 stick) unsalted butter
a pinch of sea salt

makes
2–3 x 6-ounce jars

how to eat
smother on a buttered baguette
or on hot crumpets

If you are using frozen berries, defrost them completely first as you don't want excess water in your curd. If using cranberries, substitute the lemon juice for 3 tablespoons of orange juice and ½ teaspoon of cinnamon while softening the fruit. If using blackberries, throw in a few juniper berries; if using raspberries, try adding a handful of chopped fresh mint, and if using blueberries, try adding a few fresh lemon thyme leaves.

- Soften the berries in a pan with the water and lemon juice on a medium heat. Depending on the berries used, this should take between 10–20 minutes. Make sure they are very soft and mushy and mash them a bit with a potato masher if necessary.
- Sieve the softened berries, discarding any seeds or skins and keeping the berry juice.
- Whisk the eggs, egg yolks, and sugar together until they are well mixed and light and frothy in texture.
- Gently melt the butter on a low heat in a medium, heavy-bottomed pan and, when completely melted, slowly pour in the egg mixture, stirring constantly, then add the berry juice.
- Continue stirring and cooking on the low heat until the mixture has thickened to a custard-like consistency. This may take up to 15 minutes but don't be tempted to increase the heat as this could scramble the eggs.
- Remove from the heat and whisk the mixture to remove any lumps.
- Ladle into warm, dry sterilized jars, filling them to about ¼ inch below the rim. Seal, leave to cool, and refrigerate.

Keeps for up to 1–2 weeks in the fridge.

rhubarb and cinnamon curd

Tart flavors always come up on top in curds and rhubarb is another of those. Try and get the vibrant pink forced rhubarb for this recipe. It's a much brighter color and makes for a much prettier curd.

1 lb forced rhubarb
¼ cup water
1 orange, zest only
1 tsp ground cinnamon
4 medium eggs, plus 2 yolks
1 cup superfine granulated sugar
½ cup (1 stick) unsalted butter

makes
2–3 x 6-ounce jars

how to eat
put on the base of a tart or sweet pie, add a few slices of roasted rhubarb and toasted slivered almonds, finish off with a dollop of whipped cream or brandy mascarpone

- Trim and roughly chop the rhubarb. Put in a medium pan with the water and soften for 15–20 minutes until it is easy to mash.
- Push the cooked rhubarb through a fine-mesh sieve to smooth out the pulp, then discard what's left in the sieve. Stir the orange zest and cinnamon into the pulp.
- Whisk the eggs, egg yolks, and sugar together until they are well mixed and light and frothy in texture.
- Gently melt the butter on a low heat in a medium, heavy-bottomed pan and, when completely melted, slowly pour in the egg mixture, stirring constantly.
- Stir through the sieved rhubarb and continue cooking and stirring on the low heat until the mixture has thickened to a custard-like consistency. This may take up to 15 minutes but don't be tempted to increase the heat as this could scramble the eggs.
- Remove from the heat and whisk the mixture to a smooth consistency.
- Ladle into warm, dry sterilized jars, filling them to about ¼ inch below the rim. Seal, leave to cool, and refrigerate.

Keeps for up to 1–2 weeks in the fridge.

tamarillos in syrup

My mother used to make these bittersweet, syrupy tamarillos for us as children. Simple and delicious, we'd have them on our Shredded Wheat. If you try this quick, easy delight and love it, try something a little more advanced like my Tamarillo Chutney (see page 38); it's so good.

8 tamarillos
½ cup granulated sugar

how to eat
on your breakfast cereal, with yogurt and granola, or spoon straight on your Shredded Wheat

- Peel the tamarillos by scoring the bottom with a cross, placing them in boiling water for 5 minutes, then dunking them in ice-cold water for 1 minute. Peel back the skin with a paring knife.
- Slice the peeled tamarillos into ¼-inch discs and put in a wide, shallow bowl. Sprinkle with the sugar, cover the bowl with plastic wrap, and leave overnight in the fridge to macerate.

Keep refrigerated for up to 1 week. Re-cover after spooning out what you need and return to the fridge.

figs in syrup

A delicious treat to sweeten up breakfast time.

1½ lbs fresh figs
3 cups granulated sugar
3 cups water

how to eat
on your breakfast cereal, with yogurt and granola, or as a dessert with flavored cream or mascarpone

- Peel the figs as if they were bananas but using a paring knife, then chop each one into eight pieces.
- Put all the ingredients together in a heavy-bottomed pan on a high heat and bring to boil.
- Reduce the heat to a simmer and cook, stirring, for 10–20 minutes until the figs are soft and the liquid has thickened to a syrup.
- Eat immediately or, once cooled, store in an airtight container and refrigerate.

Keeps for up to 1 week in the fridge.

candied almonds

This simple and tasty snack is sweet yet relatively healthy. Much better to have around the house than a chocolate bar or chips.

4 tbsp honey
½ tsp ground cinnamon
¼ tsp ground ginger
1½ cups whole almonds
2 tbsp raw sugar
1½ tsp sea salt

how to eat
in the school lunch box, or keep in a sweet jar for whenever you like

- Preheat the oven to 320°F.
- Warm the honey, cinnamon, and ginger in a large pan on a low heat, stirring until well combined. Add the almonds and mix until they are completely coated.
- Remove from the heat, sprinkle in the sugar and sea salt, and mix gently.
- Line a very large baking tray with baking parchment and spread the sugar-coated almonds on it in an even layer.
- Bake for 15–20 minutes, checking intermittently, until toasted and to your taste. Be careful not to overcook them: when too caramelized, they tend to taste bitter.
- Store in a large jar or an airtight container in the cupboard or on your work desk for whenever you want a snack.

candied rose petals

Candied rose petals make the most beautiful edible decorations, destined to prettify any cake or pudding you sprinkle them on. The only tools you need are a soft bristle paintbrush and a wire rack—it is so easy. You can use rose petals from your garden, foraged, or bought online—just be sure they are free from pesticides.

edible roses
1–2 egg whites
superfine granulated sugar

season late spring to summer

how to eat
as edible decoration on top of
a pavlova or Victoria sponge cake

- Very carefully pluck the individual edible petals from unsprayed roses.
- Gently wash the petals, trying not to bruise them, then leave them on kitchen paper until completely dry.
- Softly paint each petal with egg white, then dip it in a small bowl of superfine granulated sugar, sprinkling on extra, if necessary, so they are totally sugar-coated.
- Space them apart on a wire cooling rack and leave until dry and hardened.

Use the same day as they will become soft and wet if left too long or if stored in a sealed container.

candied citrus peel

Colorful and delicious, these are easy to make and are a fun gift for children and adults alike. Add to recipes that ask for candied peel such as Christmas puddings or cookies. The method is the same, whichever citrus fruits you use, so use a mixture to vary the colors and tartness. If you keep them in a sealed container they last for ages.

4–5 citrus fruits: oranges, lemons, limes, bergamots, grapefruit, kaffir limes, blood oranges, mandarin oranges
1 bag granulated sugar (about 9⅓ cups)
¼ lb dark chocolate (optional)

how to eat
straight from the container for a burst of sweetness, or put in colorful sweet bags with homemade labels and give as gifts

For a decadent version, gently melt dark chocolate in a small pan, half dip the candied peels into it, then put them on a lined wire rack and leave to set.

- Slice each fruit into 8 wedges and remove the flesh so you are left with around ¼-inch-thick pieces of peel (with the pith still on). Cut each wedge into ¼-inch-wide strips.
- Put the peel into a medium, heavy-bottomed pan and cover with cold water. Bring to boil, then simmer for 5 minutes.
- Drain the liquid, then re-cover the peel with fresh cold water, bring back to boil, and this time simmer for about 30–40 minutes.
- Drain again, keeping the peel-infused water.
- Preheat the oven to the lowest possible setting.
- Measure the peel-infused water, then add ⅓ cup of sugar to every ⅓ cup of liquid. Put in the pan over a low heat, stir until the sugar dissolves, then bring it slowly to boil and add the peel.
- Simmer for 30 minutes, until the peel has softened and appears translucent, then leave to cool in the liquid for 10 minutes off the heat.
- Line a baking tray with baking parchment and, when the peel has cooled slightly, remove it from the sugar syrup with a slotted spoon and space it out evenly on the tray. Dry-bake in the center of the oven for 30 minutes.
- Remove from the oven, fill a bowl with sugar, then toss the peel in it a few bits at a time until they are completely coated.
- Line another tray with baking parchment and evenly space the sugar-coated peel on it, leaving it to air-dry for at least 1 hour.
- Eat immediately or store in an airtight container. The candied peel will keep for at least 3–4 months.

candied kumquats

Sometimes called a Chinese orange, the earliest reference to kumquats appears in Chinese literature in the twelfth century. Vibrant and tangy, with a soft skin that you can eat, these little guys arrive when there is very little seasonal fruit on offer in late winter and early spring. So, if you are quick to react, you can get them macerating in time for the most delicious festive treat.

1 lb kumquats
1¼ cups granulated sugar
1 cinnamon stick
1 star anise
1½ tbsp sweet vermouth

makes
2 x 8-ounce jars

season late winter to early spring

how to eat
instead of biscotti with coffee. Pop into the bottom of a glass of prosecco, or half dip in melted chocolate

- Cut the thinnest slice you can off the stem end of each kumquat (this prevents the insides from popping out while cooking), then prick each one once or twice with a needle or toothpick.
- Put the kumquats in a medium, heavy-bottomed pan, cover with cold water, then bring to boil. Reduce the heat and simmer for 5 minutes, then drain.
- Cover again with cold water, bring it back to boil, and repeat the same step. Repeat this process 3 more times (5 in total) until the kumquats have softened.
- The last time, reserve ½ cup of the drained cooking water, put it in a clean, heavy-bottomed pan and add the sugar and spices. Simmer on a moderate heat, stirring until the sugar dissolves.
- Add the vermouth and kumquats, bring to boil, then lower the heat so that the mixture is just simmering and reduce for about 30 minutes. Be careful because the candy may bubble up while it thickens.
- Once reduced, remove from the heat, spoon the mixture into warm, dry sterilized jars and seal.

Keeps unopened for up to 6 months. Once opened, refrigerate and eat within 2 months.

lilac sugar

When it is in season in the springtime, try and get your hands on some edible lilac. You can find local suppliers online or, failing that, you could grow it yourself. These small but perfectly formed bright sugared tubes look particularly beautiful when used to decorate the top of a layer cake: stir the floral sugar through buttercream or sprinkle it over glaze for a fragrant and elegant mauve finish.

edible lilac flowers
granulated sugar

season late spring

how to eat
stir into a cupcake icing, or
sprinkle on top of ice cream

If lilac is out of season, there are a lot of other edible flowers you can play around with like fresh lavender or cornflowers. Make sure you get your edible flowers from a reputable source, preferably organically grown without pesticides, so they are safe to eat.

- Wash the lilac and leave to dry on kitchen paper. The flowers need to be completely dry so leave for 1-2 hours to be certain.
- Weigh the dry lilac flowers, then mix with the same weight of sugar. Stir gently until mixed well.
- Store in a large, clean dry jar and seal.

Best to use on the day it's made or, at most, within 2-3 days.

fruit leathers

If you are after a healthy-meets-sweet snack to put in your or your children's lunch box, then this is the recipe for you. Homemade fruit leathers (sometimes called roll-ups) are sticky, sweet, chewy, and nutritious. Unlike their store-bought equivalents, they are not drenched in sugar; I recommend adding just a little to taste, but you could leave it out altogether. The other joy of making leathers yourself is creating your own flavor pairings: think one fruit and one enhancing herb or spice—the rest is up to you.

peach and lavender

6 peaches
2 tbsp lemon juice
2 tsp edible lavender flowers
$\frac{1}{4}$–$\frac{1}{3}$ cup sugar or honey, to taste

apple and cinnamon

4 apples
2 tbsp lemon juice
2 tsp ground cinnamon
$\frac{1}{4}$–$\frac{1}{3}$ cup sugar or honey, to taste

pear and rosemary

6 pears
2 tbsp lemon juice
1 tsp finely chopped fresh rosemary leaves
$\frac{1}{4}$–$\frac{1}{3}$ cup sugar or honey, to taste

strawberry and mint

2 lbs fresh strawberries
2 tbsp lemon juice
2 tsp finely chopped fresh mint leaves
$\frac{1}{4}$–$\frac{1}{3}$ cup sugar or honey, to taste

makes
**4-6 strips (depending on which size
you choose)**

how to eat
as an afternoon snack, or put in
a school lunch box

Use whatever fruit is in abundance; these are
perfect for using up fruit that is a bit old and
going to waste.

- Prepare the fruit: rinse, dry, pit, peel, core, hull,
  and chop as necessary.
- Preheat the oven to the lowest possible setting.
- Blend the raw prepped fruit in a blender or
  a food processor until it is a purée. Stir in the
  lemon juice and herb or spice, and sugar or
  honey to your taste if you're using it.
- Line a large baking tray with baking parchment
  and spread the purée out evenly until you get
  a square of about 12 x 12 inches.
- Put in the center of the oven and dry-bake
  for about 6–8 hours or until the mixture is not
  gooey or sticky but just slightly tacky to the
  touch.
- Remove from the oven and leave to cool
  completely before using a ruler and sharp
  knife or a pizza cutter to slice into even strips.
- Peel away the parchment and store in an
  airtight container with new baking parchment
  separating the layers.

Keeps for up to 4 months.

apple and sage butter

Sage and apple have a long history as a support act to other dishes; here they get to have a duet. The result is heavenly on grainy toast.

2 lbs apples (gala, braeburn, or fuji)
3 fresh sage leaves
¾ cup water
2 cups granulated sugar
2 tbsp lemon juice
¼ tsp ground ginger

makes
3–4 x 8-ounce jars

how to eat
on grainy toast, or try as an alternative fruity filling for a layer cake instead of butter icing

- Peel and core the apples, discarding the scraps (or keeping them for homemade Fermented Fruit Vinegar (see page 104)) and chop roughly. Finely chop the sage.
- Put the apples and water in a large, heavy-bottomed pan and bring to a simmer for about 20 minutes until they have softened and become mushy.
- Take off the heat, cool, then blend to a purée in a food mill, blender, or a food processor.
- Return the puréed apple to the heavy-bottomed pan and bring to a gentle simmer. Add the sugar, stirring until it dissolves, then stir in the lemon juice and ginger.
- Simmer on a low heat, stirring constantly for about 30–40 minutes, until the mixture begins to hold its shape on a spoon.
- Stir in the chopped sage and infuse for another 5 minutes off the heat.
- Ladle into warm, dry sterilized jars, filling them to about ¼ inch below the rim, and seal.

Keeps unopened for up to 6 months. Once opened, refrigerate and eat within 4 weeks.

maple roasted almond butter

Not strictly a preserve but I had to include this recipe. Almonds are high in monounsaturated fats (one of the good fats) and in vitamin E so this is tasty and nourishing.

1½ cups whole almonds
3 tbsp maple syrup or honey
½ tsp sea salt
2–3 tbsp walnut, beechnut,
**   or coconut oil**

makes
2 x 6-ounce jars

how to eat
smothered on toast or, like my husband likes to do, spoon it straight from the jar

- Preheat the oven to 320°F.
- Toss the almonds in a bowl with the maple syrup, then put on a baking tray lined with baking parchment. Bake in the middle of the oven for about 20 minutes, giving them a stir halfway through, until the nuts have browned and the syrup has darkened a bit. Remove from the oven.
- Allow the nuts to cool, break into pieces, and put into a food processor or blender with any bits of hardened syrup.
- Add the salt, pulse a few times, then start drizzling in the oil slowly, using a spatula to scrape the mixture down every so often, and continue pulsing and blending until you get a buttery consistency.
- Spoon into warm, dry sterilized jars and seal.

Keeps unopened for up to 8 weeks. Once opened, refrigerate and eat within 4 weeks.

damson plum and rosemary cheese

Fruit cheeses are a thicker-set preserve than jam so they are best made with high-pectin fruits, like the damson plums in this recipe. Because of their hard set, you can have fun with presentation, using molds or cutting out shapes. Go vintage shopping and find some old jelly molds to give fruit cheeses a new lease of life.

2 lbs damson plums (fresh or frozen)
water to cover
about 2–2¼ cups granulated sugar
1 tbsp roughly chopped fresh
 rosemary leaves
3 tbsp lemon juice
butter, for greasing the muffin
 tray/molds

season late summer

how to eat
after dinner, with cheese

- Put the plums in a large, heavy-bottomed pan, cover completely with cold water and bring to boil. Reduce the heat and simmer on a low heat for 40–60 minutes, stirring intermittently. The fruit will become soft and the stones will pop out.
- When soft enough, take off the heat, cool and push through a sieve, discarding the stones and skins.
- Measure the fruit purée, then put it into a large, heavy-bottomed pan and heat gently. Add ¾ cup of sugar for every 1 cup of purée (so approximately 2 cups sugar for 2 cups puree) to the warmed purée and stir until the sugar has dissolved.
- Add the lemon juice, bring to boil and stir constantly for about 30–40 minutes, until the mixture thickens to a paste and it begins to hold its shape on a spoon. Stir through the rosemary.
- Preheat the oven to the lowest possible setting.
- Lightly butter a muffin tray or individual shaped molds and fill with the paste, leaving a ⅓-inch space at the top of each one, then level with a spatula.
- Put in the oven to dry-bake for 30–40 minutes.
- When slightly wobbly (they will harden when cool), remove from the oven and leave to cool completely before gently easing them from their molds. Eat immediately or store as below.

Keeps in an airtight container in the fridge for up to 6 months. Once opened, keep refrigerated and eat within 4 weeks.

red currant and lime cheese

Not all fruit cheeses need to be set in molds. Sometimes it's a lovely alternative to put them in jars so they can be given as a gift with personalized labels. They also keep longer this way, because the jars are sterilized.

3 lbs red currants
½ cup water
1¾ cups granulated sugar
¼ cup lime juice (about 2 limes)
⅔ cup red wine
3 limes, zest

makes
5 x 3-ounce jars

how to eat
with cheese

- Put the red currants in a large, heavy-bottomed pan with the water, bring to boil, then simmer on a low heat for 30–40 minutes until soft.
- Once soft, remove from the heat, mash the currants with a potato masher, then push through a fine-mesh sieve with a spoon to separate the pulp from the skins. Discard the skins.
- Return the pulp to the large pan, add the sugar, and heat gently, stirring until the sugar dissolves.
- Add the lime juice and bring to a simmer, stirring constantly for 20 minutes, removing any scum that forms.
- Mix in the red wine, bring to boil and then cook, stirring intermittently, until it has reduced in volume by half and the mixture begins to hold its shape on a spoon.
- Remove the pan from the heat and skim off any remaining scum. Stir through the lime zest.
- Ladle into warm, dry sterilized jars, filling them to about ¼ inch below the rim, and seal.

Keeps unopened for up to a year. Once opened, refrigerate and eat within 3 months.

salt and pepper plum cheese

It's nice to have sweet things with cheese, and fruit cheeses definitely serve this purpose. The sweet acidity of plums beautifully balances the salty fattiness of cheese and, with a little salt and pepper in the mix, it's a fun match.

2 lbs red plums
½ vanilla pod
⅔ cup water
10 black peppercorns
about 2–2¼ cups granulated sugar
3 tbsp lemon juice
½ tsp sea salt

makes
5 x 3-ounce jars

how to eat
with cheese

- Cut the plums in half, remove the pits, then wrap the stones in a square of muslin and tie this into a bag with kitchen string (the stones add pectin and flavor to the preserve).
- Split the vanilla pod lengthwise, remove the seeds, and keep both.
- Put the prepared plums and muslin bag in a large, heavy-bottomed pan with the vanilla seeds, vanilla pod, water, and peppercorns, and bring to boil.
- Simmer on a low heat, stirring constantly, for 30–40 minutes, making sure the mixture doesn't stick to the bottom of the pan.
- When the plums are soft, take off the heat and push them through a fine-mesh sieve, discarding the skins, muslin bag, vanilla pod, and peppercorns.
- Measure the fruit purée and put it into a large, heavy-bottomed pan. Add 1 cup sugar for every 1 cup of puree, then gently heat the mixture and stir until the sugar has dissolved.
- Add the lemon juice, bring to boil, then simmer gently for another 30–40 minutes, stirring intermittently, until thickened and the mixture begins to hold its shape on a spoon.
- Remove from the heat and stir through the salt, then ladle into warm, dry sterilized jars, filling them to about ¼ inch below the rim, and seal.

Keeps unopened for up to 6 months. Once opened, refrigerate and eat within 4 weeks.

membrillo

A Spanish quince paste similar to an English fruit cheese, this delicacy is mostly eaten with hard cheese, especially Spanish Manchego. Newton & Pott's stall on Broadway Market is next to the best Spanish deli stall, Santos & Santos. Manuel, the owner, has an impeccable palate when it comes to food from the Mediterranean. He has tasted my membrillo and, after a few attempts, I have got his official nod.

3 lbs quinces
1 vanilla pod
1 lemon, peel and juice
about 2–2½ cups granulated sugar
butter, for greasing the pan/mold

season early winter to early spring

how to eat
slice and wrap in baking parchment, tie with string, and take to a dinner party as a gift with some Manchego cheese

For variation and extra flavor, stir in roughly chopped fresh herbs like rosemary or lemon thyme leaves just before pouring it into the pan. Use apples instead, if you can't find quinces or you have an abundance of them.

- Peel, core, and roughly chop the quinces, split the vanilla pod lengthwise, and remove the seeds, and peel the lemon with a vegetable peeler.
- Put the prepared quinces in a large pan with the vanilla pod, vanilla seeds, and lemon peel. Completely cover with cold water, bring to boil, then simmer for 30–40 minutes until the quinces are tender.
- Drain off the water, discarding the vanilla pod but keeping the lemon peel.
- Blend the quinces and lemon peel to a purée using a food processor or blender.
- Weigh the purée, then put it into a large, heavy-bottomed pan and heat gently.
- For every 1 cup of purée, add ¾ cup of sugar to the pan, then stir until the sugar has dissolved.
- Add the lemon juice and cook over a low heat, stirring occasionally, for 1–1½ hours.
- The mixture will thicken a lot, turn a deep pinky color, and start to hold its shape on a spoon.
- Preheat the oven to the lowest possible setting.
- Line and grease a loaf tin or Pyrex dish of about 8 x 8 inches. Pour in the quince paste, level the top with a spatula, then put in the oven to dry-bake for 40–60 minutes.
- Once set, remove from the oven, leave to cool completely, and then gently ease the membrillo from its mold. Eat immediately or store as below.

Keeps for up to 6 months in an airtight container in the fridge.

pear, wine, and fennel seed butter

Not soft enough to be a jam, thick and spreadable like a butter, yet not quite hard enough to be a fruit cheese… this is the loveliness that is a fruit butter.

1 ½ lbs pears
⅓ cup water
⅓ cup medium white wine
2 tbsp lemon juice
1 ½ cups granulated sugar
¼ tsp ground cinnamon
¾ tsp fennel seeds

makes
2–3 x 8-ounce jars

season winter to early spring

how to eat
scrumptious on a toasted English muffin

- Peel, core, and roughly chop the pears.
- Put the pears and water in a large, heavy-bottomed pan and bring to a simmer for about 15–20 minutes, until the pears have softened and become mushy.
- Cool slightly, then blend the mixture to a purée in a food mill, blender, or a food processor.
- Return the puréed pear to the heavy-bottomed pan, add the wine, lemon juice, and sugar, then simmer, stirring, until the sugar dissolves.
- Add the cinnamon and fennel seeds and continue to simmer, stirring intermittently, for about 40–50 minutes.
- Once thickened and the mixture begins to hold its shape on a spoon, take off the heat, ladle into warm, dry sterilized jars, filling them to about ¼ inch below the rim, and seal.

Keeps unopened for up to 6 months. Once opened, refrigerate and eat within 4 weeks.

peach and toasted almond butter

A fun alternative spread with a bit of crunch. If you can't decide whether it's a jam or a nut butter you want on your toast this morning, why not have both? The combination of sweet luscious peach flavor with a bitter toasted almond bite is a delight and the best of both worlds.

2 lbs peaches
1½ cups granulated sugar
2 tbsp lemon juice (about ½ lemon)
⅓ cup water
1 lemon, zest
¼ tsp ground cinnamon
2 tbsp slivered almonds

makes
2–3 x 8-ounce jars

how to eat
on buttered grainy toast

You need to start this recipe the day before you want to make the butter. To peel the peaches, score a cross on the bottom, dip them into boiling water for 1–2 minutes, then dunk them in an ice-cold water bath. Then simply slip off the skins.

- Roughly chop the peaches and discard the stones.
- Toss the fruit with the sugar and lemon juice in a large bowl, transfer to an airtight container, and leave in the fridge to macerate overnight.
- The next day, put the sugar-soaked peaches in a large, heavy-bottomed pan with the water, lemon zest, and cinnamon and bring to boil.
- Reduce the heat to a gentle simmer, stirring occasionally to make sure it doesn't burn on the bottom, and cook for 20–30 minutes until it has a thick paste-like consistency.
- Meanwhile, gently toast the slivered almonds in a small frying pan until they are golden brown, then stir them through the peach pulp and cook for another 5 minutes.
- Once thickened and the mixture begins to hold its shape on a spoon, take off the heat, ladle into warm, dry sterilized jars, filling them to about ¼ inch below the rim, and seal.

Keeps unopened for up to 6 months. Once opened, refrigerate and eat within 4 weeks.

syrups, cordials, and alcohol

Naughty and nice. Let's start with nice. In this chapter there are simple recipes for delicious syrups and cordials, which are great substitutes for the sugary fizzy drinks that are on the market. Add a wee jot to hot or cold water, fizzy or still, and you'll have no more need for those devilish soft drinks.

As for naughty, the boozy, fruity tipples here are fun to make, give, mix, and, of course, drink. At my place, we make a lot of cocktails and people are always impressed at what we can quickly throw together for a surprise guest. It helps when there's a preserver in the house.

syrups and cordials

By adding a little sugar to fruit, herbs, or flowers, boiling or steeping
to soften and help draw out the essence, then straining through muslin
or a fine-mesh sieve, you can create a fruit, herbal, or floral concentrate.
This can be mixed, drizzled, and diluted into and onto a number of different
delights from cakes, to ice cream, to cocktails. And why not encourage
your kids away from sugar by diluting a fruit concentrate, then freezing
it into popsicle molds. What a treat, and healthier than any store-bought
alternative.

alcohol

Fruit and alcohol come together here in various different recipes from
simple, fruit-steeped alcohols to more ambitious liqueurs infused with
fruit syrups. Both take some time so be prepared: They might not be
ready for this weekend's house party but, since alcohol is a great
preservative, they last for a few years, so you will have them for plenty
of other celebrations.

In this chapter, we find sugar, plus a variety of natural flavorings such
as flowers, herbs, and spices, are often added to help the fruit macerate,
so there are plenty of fun cocktail combinations to experiment with.
And, although they make delicious cocktails, these alcohols are equally
tasty served straight or with ice. Like their non-alcoholic counterparts,
they can also be used in baking and general cooking, as suggested in
specific recipes.

key ingredients

Fruit, sugar, alcohol/spirits, herbs, flowers, and spices are the basics.

Fruit: The fruit that goes into syrups, cordials, and alcohols can be newly picked, ripe, or even frozen in some cases. If you have fruit that is too ripe to use for jam, then use it for one of these recipes instead.

Sugar: It is best to use refined white granulated and superfine granulated sugars in this chapter. White sugar doesn't influence flavor whereas brown or raw unrefined sugars can dominate it or dull the vibrant fruity colors.

Alcohol/spirits: Use high-proof spirits (35% plus alcohol content) that are low in flavor such as gin and vodka. Whisky and brandy work well in some recipes but keep in mind the barrel-aged flavor when playing around with your own concoctions as this will affect the final taste.

Herbs/flowers/spices: You can use fresh and dried. They introduce flavor and, since this can be quite overpowering, experiment using a little at a time. Basically, don't overdo it.

key equipment

- Several large 1–3 liter jars with lids: for steeping the tinctures.
- Collection of sterilized bottles, corks, caps, and lids.
- Muddle/flat-ended rolling pin: for mashing or breaking down the fruit.
- A large, heavy-bottomed stainless steel pan: for softening fruit and warming.
- Wooden spoons with long handles.
- Blender, food processor, or a food mill: for puréeing some fruits.
- Large muslin squares and kitchen string or jelly bags: for drip-sieving juices.
- Fine-mesh sieve: for straining the essence from the fruits.
- Muslin squares: for a finer, purer strain.
- Measuring jug and weighing scales.
- Funnels—one with a wide, short spout and another with a long, thin spout: for bottling.
- Ladle and spatula: for spooning out the liquids and scraping out the remains.
- Baking parchment and a large baking tray: to dehydrate some fruit.

method tips

- Use fresh and ripe seasonal fruit, wash, discard any fruit that has spoiled or is damaged or mushy. Then prepare as appropriate: peel, hull, de-stalk, core, then chop or slice as per the recipe. Sometimes the seeds or pits are discarded, sometimes not as they carry some of the flavors but the recipes will guide you through the individual procedures for the different types of fruits. If using citrus fruits, it's best to use unwaxed fruits, as sometimes it's the skins and peel (i.e. the whole fruits) that are used in this chapter.

- Macerate as long as the recipe suggests for flavorsome infusions; you may need to be patient with some of them.

- For recipes that require straining boiled, or pulped fruits (and most syrups and cordials do), tie it up into a large piece of muslin with some kitchen string, or into a store-bought jelly bag. Place a catch bowl underneath and leave to strain overnight, or for at least 8 hours. Resist squeezing the fruit-filled bag and allow it to drip at its own speed; squeezing it will make the liquid cloudy, whereas leaving it to strain naturally will produce a lovely clear juice. Discard the leftover pulp, or you can use it to make a healthy snack like Fruit Leathers (see page 218).

- For a clearer result without sediment, strain the liquid a few times through clean muslin or a store-bought jelly bag, or line a fine-mesh sieve with two layers of muslin.

- Clean and sterilize everything: pan, ladle, funnel, jug, jars, bottles, and lids (see page 13 for the method), and make sure your jars, bottles and lids are completely dry before filling. By cleaning and sterilizing your kit properly, the preserves will keep for longer.

- With most of the alcohol-based recipes, leave the sterilized bottles to cool a little before filling them.

- Syrups and cordials should be poured while still moderately hot into warm, sterilized and completely dry bottles, then sealed immediately. If you do this correctly they should keep for up to 4–8 months in a cupboard unopened; once opened, store in the fridge and use within 4–6 weeks.

- Alcohol infusions/liqueurs should be strained through a fine-mesh sieve (sometimes lined with muslin, and more than once) before being poured into dry, sterilized bottles, then sealed tightly.

G.S. STIRLING
CHEMIST

homemade lemonade/limeade

Refreshing and sweetly tart. Quick and simple to make.

2 lemons or limes
½ cup superfine granulated sugar
6⅓ cups water
ice
lemon or lime slices, to decorate

makes
2-liter jug

how to drink
all lemonades are best enjoyed when
you just can't take the heat anymore
and deserve a nice tall ice-cold,
refreshing liquid treat

- Cut the lemons or limes into eighths,
  removing and discarding any seeds.
- Blend the citrus fruits with the sugar and
  3⅓ cups of the water in a blender or a
  food processor until the fruit is completely
  pulverised and the mixture is foamy
  and whitish.
- Strain the mixture through a fine-mesh
  sieve into a large jug filled with ice, pouring
  the remainder of the water through as well.
  Discard what's left in the sieve.
- Decorate with the citrus slices and
  drink immediately.

homemade strawberry lemonade

Low in sugar, high in taste. Summer in a jug.

1 lb strawberries, plus ¼ lb extra for
**   decoration**
⅓ cup lemon juice
4¼ cups water
½ cup superfine granulated sugar or
**   1 cup honey**
ice

makes
1.5-liter jug

how to drink
(see above)

- Halve 1¾ cups of the strawberries and slice
  the remaining ⅓ cup for the garnish.
- Blitz the halved strawberries, lemon juice,
  1¾ cups of the water and the sugar or honey
  together in a blender or a food processor.
- Strain the mixture through a fine-mesh sieve
  into a large jug filled with ice, pouring the
  remainder of the water through as well.
  Discard what's left in the sieve.
- Decorate with the sliced strawberries.
  Drink immediately.

peach and basil lemonade

Deliciously tarty, delightfully peachy, and such a gorgeous color!

2 large peaches
4¼ cups water
¾ cup granulated sugar
⅓ cup lemon juice
5–8 basil leaves (or to your taste)
ice
basil sprigs, to decorate

makes
1.5-liter jug

how to drink
(see page 238)

The peaches need peeling for this recipe. Do this by cutting a cross on their base, blanching them in boiling water for a couple of minutes, then dunking them in ice-cold water. The skins will peel off very easily.

- Roughly chop the peaches and discard the stones.
- Bring the peaches, 1¾ cups of the water, and the sugar to boil in a small, heavy-bottomed pan, then lower the heat and simmer for 5 minutes, stirring, to soften the fruit and dissolve the sugar.
- Remove from the heat and allow to cool before putting the mixture in a blender or a food processor with the lemon juice and basil and blitzing it.
- Strain through a fine-mesh sieve into a large jug full of ice, pouring the remainder of the water through as well. Discard what's left in the sieve.
- Decorate with the basil sprigs and drink immediately.

cranberry, orange, and maple syrup

This is a nice syrup to make in winter and it helps combat any seasonal lethargy.
Cranberries are renowned for their antioxidant qualities and, what with the vitamin C
in orange and the natural sweetness of maple, you'll feel the difference immediately.

1 lb cranberries
1 orange, zest and juice (you need
    about ¼ cup juice)
3⅓ cups water
½ cup granulated sugar
⅔ cup maple syrup or honey

makes
2–3 x 8-ounce bottles

how to drink
mix with iced still or sparkling water
to your taste. Serve in a hot toddy
to keep winter bugs at bay

- Put the cranberries, orange zest, and water
  in a large pan, bring to boil, then lower the heat
  and simmer for about 10–15 minutes until the
  cranberries start to pop.
- Remove from the heat, gently mash with a
  potato masher, then strain through a jelly bag or
  muslin into a bowl (see page 236) overnight or
  for up to 8 hours. Resist squeezing the fruit-
  filled bag as this will make the liquid cloudy.
- Measure 3 cups of the juice for this recipe and
  freeze any spare juice for another day. Put the
  juice in a large, heavy-bottomed pan with the
  sugar and maple syrup, bring to boil, stirring to
  dissolve the sugar, lower to a simmer, and
  stir for another 15–20 minutes until the liquid
  reduces slightly and thickens to a syrupy
  consistency.
- Stir in the orange juice and simmer for
  another 2 minutes, then take off the heat.
- Skim off any scum from the surface, strain
  through a fine-mesh sieve, then pour into
  warm, dry sterilized bottles and seal.

Keeps unopened for up to 4 months. Once
opened, keep in the fridge and use within
4–6 weeks.

quince and blood orange syrup

Such a pretty colored drink. Use it to design your own cocktail!

4–5 quinces
water to cover
3–4 blood oranges (you need
  ¾ cup juice)
½ tsp coriander seeds
1½ cups granulated sugar

makes
1 x 17-ounce bottle

how to drink
use to replace sugary, soft drinks
in your life. Syrups mixed with fizzy
water are a much healthier alternative

- Roughly chop the quinces, put in a large stockpot, and cover with water so that when you push down with your palm on the quinces your hand is completely submerged. Boil rapidly, stirring intermittently, for 1½–2 hours until they are soft and mushy.
- Remove from the heat, mash with a potato masher and strain through a jelly bag or muslin into a bowl (see page 236) for up to 8 hours. Resist squeezing the fruit-filled bag as this will make the liquid cloudy.
- Measure 1½ cups of the juice for this recipe and freeze the rest for another day.
- Juice the blood oranges and reserve.
- Crush the coriander seeds using a mortar and pestle, then put with the measured quince juice and the sugar in a large, heavy-bottomed pan and heat gently, stirring to dissolve the sugar. Simmer for 8–10 minutes. It will want to boil up and foam but continual stirring will stop this.
- Remove from the heat, stir in the blood orange juice, then return to the heat and bring back to a simmer for another 2 minutes. Remove from the heat.
- Skim off any scum from the surface, strain through a fine-mesh sieve, then pour into the warm, dry sterilized bottle and seal.

Keeps unopened for up to 4 months. Once opened, keep in the fridge and use within 4 weeks.

CRANBERRY
& MAPLE SYRU

UP
RHUBA
SY
TAMARI
SYRU

basil/mint syrup

Drizzling either of these flavors onto ice cream is a decadent treat. I love basil syrup on dark chocolate ice cream, or alternatively, mint syrup on raspberry and white chocolate ice cream; both are easy but impressive desserts to surprise guests with.

½ cup fresh basil or mint
3 tbsp lemon juice
1½ cups granulated sugar
1 tsp sea salt
3⅓ cups boiling water

makes
1 x 17-ounce bottle

how to eat/drink
add to cocktails, with or without alcohol. Also lovely spooned onto a cake fresh from the oven

Ensure the basil or mint is completely dry after washing and prepping, patting dry with paper towels if necessary.

- Put the herb with the lemon juice into a mortar or a large bowl, then muddle them together using the pestle (or use a flat-ended rolling pin if using a bowl).
- Add the sugar and salt, muddle a little more, then stir in the measured boiling water and leave covered overnight or for at least 8–10 hours to macerate.
- Strain the juice through a muslin-lined fine-mesh sieve into a medium, heavy-bottomed pan.
- Slowly bring the sieved juice to boil, then lower the heat and simmer, stirring intermittently, for 20–30 minutes, or until it becomes syrupy in consistency and has reduced by a third.
- Remove from the heat. Skim off any scum from the surface then pour into the warm, dry sterilized bottle and seal.

Keeps unopened for up to 4 months. Once opened, keep in the fridge and use within 4–6 weeks.

pineapple and chili syrup

Sweet with a hint of spice, this is an exciting and unexpected flavor. The exotic tones of pineapple make it cool and refreshing while the chili makes it warming and cozy. It works both with iced fizzy water, as a summer drink, or in a mug of hot water as a winter warmer. You can make different densities, depending on how you want to use it—for example, make a light syrup for cocktail mixes or a heavy one for drizzling on ice cream.

1 large pineapple
2 Thai chilis
1½ cups water

for 2½ cups liquid
light syrup—½ cup granulated sugar
medium syrup—1 cup granulated sugar
heavy syrup—1¼ cups granulated sugar

makes
1 x 17-ounce bottle

how to drink/eat
as a hot or cold drink, or drizzle over coconut ice cream or a coconut cake fresh out of the oven

- Peel and roughly chop the pineapple into ⅓–¾-inch pieces, roughly chop the chilis.
- Put the pineapple, chilis, and water in a medium, heavy-bottomed pan and bring to a simmer for 15–20 minutes until the fruit softens.
- Remove from the heat, allow to cool slightly, then blitz to a purée in a food processor or a blender.
- Strain the purée through a jelly bag or large muslin square into a bowl (see page 236) for up to 8 hours. Resist squeezing the fruit-filled bag as this will make the liquid cloudy.
- Measure the juice, pour it into a large, heavy-bottomed pan, then add the required amount of sugar, depending on whether you want a light, medium, or heavy syrup.
- Slowly bring to boil on a moderate heat, stirring to dissolve the sugar, then lower the heat to a simmer and reduce the liquid, stirring intermittently, for 20–30 minutes, until it becomes syrupy in consistency.
- Remove from the heat. Skim off any scum from the surface then pour into the sterilized bottle and seal.

Keeps unopened for up to 6 months. Once opened, keep in the fridge and use within 4–6 weeks.

tamarillo syrup

As you may already know I really like tamarillos. Whether it's the childhood memory of having them as a breakfast delicacy (see page 204) or that bittersweet combination that pleases my palate so much. Try the light syrup in a cocktail as follows: 1 part lemon juice, 2 parts light tamarillo syrup, 2 parts vodka, shake over ice, then half-fill a champagne glass and top up with prosecco. It's delish! Tamarillos are uniquely special and I just love them.

8–10 tamarillos
1¼ cups water
3 tbsp lemon juice

for 2 cups liquid
light syrup—granulated ½ cup sugar
medium syrup—¾ cup granulated sugar
heavy syrup—1 cup granulated sugar

makes
1–2 x 8-ounce bottles

how to drink
light syrup—in a bespoke cocktail; medium syrup—poured over a freshly baked cheesecake; heavy syrup—as a topping for lime or coconut ice cream

- Peel the tamarillos by scoring the bottom with a cross, placing them in boiling water for 5 minutes, then dunking them in ice-cold water for 1 minute. Peel back the skin with a paring knife and chop roughly.
- Put the prepped tamarillos and water in a medium, heavy-bottomed pan, bring to boil, then lower the heat and simmer for 15–25 minutes until the fruit is soft and mushy. Lightly mash with a potato masher to break up a little more.
- Remove from the heat. Strain the mixture through a jelly bag or large muslin square into a bowl (see page 236) and leave for 6–8 hours. Resist squeezing the fruit-filled bag as this will make the liquid cloudy.
- Measure the tamarillo juice, pour it into a large, heavy-bottomed pan with the lemon juice, then add the required amount of sugar, depending on whether you want a light, medium, or heavy syrup.
- Slowly bring to boil on a medium heat, stirring to dissolve the sugar, then lower the heat to a simmer and reduce the liquid, stirring intermittently, for 20–30 minutes, until it becomes syrupy in consistency.
- Take off the heat. Skim off any scum from the surface then pour into warm, dry sterilized bottles and seal.

Keeps unopened for up to 4 months. Once opened, keep in the fridge and use within 4 weeks.

orange and cardamom cordial

Adding herbs and spices to cordials gives them a great kick. I'm a lover of things like ginger and wasabi, so I appreciate fresh, lively bursts of flavor.

**zest of 2 oranges and juice of 8
 oranges (you need 2 cups of juice)**
5 green cardamom pods
1½ cups water
1¾ cups granulated sugar

makes
2 x 17-ounce bottles

how to drink
mix with still or sparkling water
to your taste

- Juice the oranges or measure out 2 cups of freshly squeezed orange juice. Lightly smash the cardamom pods with the blade of a knife.
- Put the water, orange zest, cardamom, and sugar in a large, heavy-bottomed pan. Simmer, stirring until the sugar has dissolved and the cardamom has infused for at least 15 minutes.
- Remove from the heat, stir in the orange juice, and then bring back to a simmer for 2 more minutes. Take off the heat once again.
- Skim off any scum from the surface, strain through a fine-mesh sieve, then pour into warm, dry sterilized bottles and seal.

Keeps unopened for up to 4 months. Once opened, keep in the fridge and use within 4–6 weeks.

rhubarb and vanilla cordial

Tart, refreshing, and delicious! Cordials are generally lighter than a syrup and are mostly used for drinking rather than adding to your cooking. Hot or cold, cordials make a great alternative to fizzy drinks.

2 lbs forced rhubarb
½ vanilla pod
3½ tbsp water
**1¼ cup superfine granulated sugar
   per 2 cups rhubarb juice**
**1 tbsp lemon juice per 2 cups
   rhubarb juice**

makes
1 x 17-ounce bottle

how to drink
mix with still or sparkling water
to your taste. Dilute and freeze
in molds to make tasty popsicles

- Roughly chop the rhubarb into ⅓–¾ inch pieces. Split open the vanilla pod lengthwise, remove the seeds, and keep both the pod and seeds.
- Put the rhubarb in a pan with the water and heat slowly. Stew for about 10–15 minutes until completely soft and mushy. Remove from the heat, mash with a potato masher, and strain through a jelly bag or muslin into a bowl overnight or for 8–10 hours (see page 236). Resist squeezing the fruit-filled bag as this will make the liquid cloudy.
- Measure the juice. Add 1¼ cups of sugar and 1 tablespoon of lemon juice to every 2 cups of rhubarb juice, put them in a large, heavy-bottomed pan, and mix through the vanilla seeds and the emptied pod.
- Heat the mixture slowly, stirring to dissolve the sugar then simmer gently for 10–15 minutes, stirring all the time, to infuse it with the vanilla.
- Take off the heat. Skim off any scum from the surface, strain through a fine-mesh sieve, then pour into the warm, dry sterilized bottle and seal.

Keeps unopened for up to 4 months. Once opened, keep in the fridge and use within 4–6 weeks.

pomegranate and apple cordial

Pomegranate seeds, those "Persian jewels," are full of nutrients and the fruit's antioxidant qualities have been well-documented. Historically, it is considered a symbol of eternal life, a good reason to start drinking this! And you don't have to go to Iran to purchase a pomegranate anymore. I love that these can now be found down at my local shop.

2–3 large pomegranates
4 large apples or 1¼ cups apple juice
3½ tbsp water
¾ cup granulated sugar
½ cup honey

makes
2 x 17-ounce bottles

how to drink
mix with still or sparkling water
to your taste

- Cut the pomegranates in half and put the halves in a bowl of water. Break the halves apart in the water, pulling the seeds from the flesh and discarding the white pith that floats to the surface. Scoop out the seeds and put aside, removing any white pith that remains.
- If necessary, juice the apples in a juicer to get 1¼ cups of fresh apple juice.
- Blitz the pomegranate seeds with the water in a blender or a food processor until it turns to juice. Measure out 3 cups of this juice then sieve it and put it into a large, heavy-bottomed pan.
- Add the apple juice, sugar, and honey, heat gently stirring to dissolve the sugar, then simmer over a low heat, stirring intermittently for about 10–15 minutes.
- Remove from the heat, skim off any scum from the surface, strain through a muslin-lined fine-mesh sieve, then pour into the warm, dry sterilized bottles and seal.

Keeps unopened for up to 4 months. Once opened, keep in the fridge and use within 4–6 weeks.

watermelon and rose cordial

Summer is full of treats and one of the fundamental pleasures of making preserves is breathing longer life into those quintessential flavors of summer. The watermelon in this cordial is a case in point. Be subtle with the rose, it's not to everyone's taste.

**1 small watermelon (to make
  4 cups juice)**
2⅓ cups superfine granulated sugar
4 tbsp lemon juice
**1–2 tsp edible dried rose petals,
  to taste**

makes
2 x 17-ounce bottles

how to drink
use to make a watermelon and rose daiquiri, an essential summer treat

- Cut the watermelon in half, scoop out the flesh, and blitz on pulse in a blender or a food processor, for about 8 pulses.
- Strain the watermelon juice through a fine-mesh sieve and discard any remaining pulp.
- Measure the juice and mix in 2 cups sugar and 4 tablespoons of lemon juice for every 4 cups of juice.
- Put the mixture into a large, heavy-bottomed pan with the desired amount of rose petals and gently bring to a simmer, stirring to dissolve the sugar.
- After 5–10 minutes of simmering, remove from the heat, strain through a muslin-lined fine-mesh sieve, then pour into warm, dry sterilized bottles and seal.

Keeps unopened for up to 4 months. Once opened, keep in the fridge and use within 4–6 weeks.

lemon verbena tea cordial

Lemon verbena, native to South America, is a magic herb that I would add to everything if I could. The fragrant lemony leaves have a huge flavor. This is great as a hot tea but even better as an iced cordial in a tall glass decorated with a sprig of mint.

2 cups loose lemon verbena whole dried leaves
4 cups boiling water
2 cups granulated sugar
⅓ cup lemon juice

makes
2–3 x 8-ounce bottles

how to drink
mix with still or sparkling water to your taste. Or play around with it in a cocktail recipe to add your own twist

- Measure the verbena leaves into a large measuring cup and fill with the boiling water to just over the 4-cup mark. Steep for 5 minutes.
- Strain the verbena-infused water through a fine-mesh sieve into a large, heavy-bottomed pan, add the sugar and lemon juice, then gently heat to a simmer.
- Stir to dissolve the sugar and simmer, stirring intermittently, for 10–15 minutes until it reduces and thickens very slightly.
- Remove from the heat and strain through a muslin-lined fine-mesh sieve, then pour into warm, dry sterilized bottles and seal.

Keeps unopened for up to 4 months. Once opened, keep in the fridge and use within 4–6 weeks.

cucumber and mint cordial

Think Edwardian picnic. Think club sandwiches and Scotch eggs. Think scones with whipped butter and jam and homemade shortbread. Think summer days laid out in the park. Think cucumber and mint cordial.

2 large cucumbers
2 large handfuls of fresh mint
1¾ cups water
2 cups granulated sugar
⅓ cup lemon juice

makes
2–3 x 8-ounce bottles

how to drink
dilute and take in a flask to a picnic. Or take cups, ice, and fizzy water instead and let everyone dilute their own to taste

- Grate the cucumbers, strip the mint leaves from the stalks (discard the stalks), then blitz them together in a blender or a food processor.
- Strain through a jelly bag or muslin into a bowl overnight or for 8–10 hours (see page 236). Resist squeezing the fruit-filled bag as this will make the liquid cloudy.
- Measure out 2½ cups of the cucumber mint juice and put it in a large, heavy-bottomed pan. Add the water, sugar, and lemon juice, heat gently, stirring to dissolve the sugar, then simmer for 10–15 minutes, stirring intermittently.
- Remove from the heat, skim off any scum from the surface, strain through a muslin-lined fine-mesh sieve, then pour into warm, dry sterilized bottles and seal.

Keeps unopened for up to 4 months. Once opened, keep in the fridge and use within 4–6 weeks.

gomme/simple syrup

You can buy gomme syrup to use in cocktails at home, but it's so simple to make and takes no time at all, that even most cocktail bars make their own. It doesn't last quite as long as the commercial alternative but at least there are no nasty additives added.

1 cup granulated sugar
2 cups water
1 tsp lemon juice

makes
1 x 17-ounce bottle
·

how to drink
add to whiskey, amaretto, or mezcal sours as well as any other cocktails that need a touch of sweetness

- Put the sugar and water into a heavy-bottomed pan and heat to a simmer without boiling. Stir intermittently for about 10–15 minutes, until the sugar is completely dissolved.
- Remove from the heat, add the lemon juice, and cool.
- Pour into a warm, dry sterilized bottle and seal.

Keeps refrigerated for up to 4 weeks

Damson
Gin 12/8

damson/sloe gin

If you can get your hands on damson plums, or sloes, or other stonefruits in mid/late summer, pick a lot to make this and other recipes, such as Damson and Rosemary Cheese (see page 224) or Damson and Orange Jam (see page 166). They freeze really well raw so you can store them to use later. Make this recipe in time to drink for Christmas, or wrap it up and give it as a gift to that uncle who likes his tipple...

1⅓ lbs damson plums or sloes (fresh or frozen)
⅔ cup superfine granulated sugar
1 tsp almond or vanilla extract (optional)
4¼ cups gin

makes
4 x 12-ounce or 2 x 1-liter bottles

how to drink
in a tumbler over ice or mixed into a champagne cocktail

- Prick the damsons/sloes with a large needle or toothpick.
- Put the damsons/sloes in a cooled, dry, sterilized large, wide-rimmed 6- to 8-cup jar and stir in the sugar. Add a teaspoon of extract if you want, cover with the gin, stir gently, and seal.
- Leave to macerate in a dark place at room temperature for up to 3 months, gently rocking the mixture daily for the first week to dissolve the sugar, then once a week thereafter.
- After this time, strain the infused gin (keeping the boozy damsons/sloes, if you like, to make a jam) through a muslin-lined fine-mesh sieve, then pour into cooled, dry sterilized bottles and seal.

Keeps for up to 1–2 years.

cranberry and lime gin

A festive tipple.

½ lb cranberries
3 limes, zest only
3⅓ tbsp lime juice (about 1–2 limes)
⅔ cup superfine granulated sugar
2½ cups gin

makes
2 x 17-ounce or 1-liter bottle

how to drink
in a tumbler with just ice or topped
up with soda water, tonic water, or
lemonade

- Prick the cranberries with a needle or toothpick.
- Put the cranberries into cooled, dry sterilized bottle/s and add the lime zest and juice (share the zest and juice between the bottles if you are using 2 bottles).
- Mix the sugar with the gin and stir to dissolve it. Fill the bottle/s to about ¾ inch from the top and seal.
- Infuse in a cool, dark place, gently rocking the gin daily, for 2 weeks or so, after which it should be ready to drink.

Keeps for up to 1–2 years if you sieve it and discard the fruit.

polish lemon vodka

The first time I met my Polish grandmother-in-law we sat down to a feast of cold meats, ćwikła (see page 72), and egg salad matched with shots of homemade versions of the traditional fruit-infused vodkas popular in Poland. It was 11am.

2 lemons, peel only
4 tsp superfine granulated sugar
4 cups vodka

makes
2 x 17-ounce or 1-liter bottle

how to drink
from the freezer in chilled shot
glasses

Variations: substitute the lemon peel with any of the following: the peel of 2 oranges, 2 stalks of lemongrass, sliced, 4 sprigs of lemon thyme, or 6 basil leaves, torn.

- Peel the lemons, scrape off as much of the white pith as you can and slice the peel into thin ¼ inch strips.
- Put the peel in a cooled, dry, sterilized, large, wide-rimmed 17-ounce jar, stir in the sugar and cover with ¾ cup of the vodka, swirl, then seal and infuse for 3–5 days in a cool, dark place.
- After this time, strain the infused alcohol through a muslin-lined fine-mesh sieve, then pour into cooled, dry sterilized bottle/s, top up with the remaining measure of vodka and seal.

Keeps for up to 1–2 years.

strawberry and lavender gin

Pretty. Delicious.

1 lb strawberries
½ vanilla pod
1 cup superfine granulated sugar
1 tsp edible dried lavender
3⅓ cups gin

makes
2 x 17-ounce or 1-liter bottle

how to drink
in a champagne cocktail, or with lemonade in a tall tumbler glass with ice

- Halve the strawberries and put them in a cooled, dry, sterilized, large, wide-rimmed 6- to 8-cup jar. Remove the seeds from the vanilla pod and keep both the pod and seeds. Stir the sugar, lavender, vanilla seeds, and pod into the strawberries, cover with the gin, give it a swirl and seal.
- Leave to macerate in a dark place at room temperature for at least 2 weeks, gently rocking the mixture daily to dissolve the sugar.
- After this time, strain the infused gin through a muslin-lined fine-mesh sieve into cooled, dry sterilized bottle/s and seal.

Keeps for up to 1–2 years.

pomegranate vodka

Vodka infused with these beautiful crimson seeds looks fabulous. We were given some of this, homemade, for Christmas and it didn't stick around for long—what a great gift.

2 large pomegranates
3⅓ cups vodka
1 cup superfine granulated sugar
¾ cup water

makes
4 x 17-ounce or 2 x 1-liter bottles

how to drink
neat in a sherry glass, or put a shot in the bottom of a flute and top up with prosecco

- Cut the pomegranates in half and put the halves in a bowl of water. Break the halves apart in the water, pulling the seeds from the flesh, and discarding the white pith that floats to the surface. Scoop out the seeds and put aside, removing any white pith that remains.
- Put the seeds in a cooled, dry, sterilized, large, wide-rimmed 6- to 8-cup jar with the vodka.
- Dissolve the sugar with the water in a heavy-bottomed pan on a moderate heat, simmer for 5 minutes. Allow to cool, then mix into the jar.
- Leave to macerate in a dark place at room temperature for up to 3 months, gently rocking the mixture daily for the first week, then once a week thereafter.
- After this time, strain the infused vodka through a muslin-lined fine-mesh sieve then pour into cooled, dry sterilized bottles and seal.

Keeps for up to 1–2 years.

crème de cassis

In our home we love cocktails—I think this derives from my university days when I worked at The Merchant Mezze bar in Auckland, New Zealand. Kirs and kir royales were on the menu there and continue to be on our menu at home to date.

1⅓ lbs blackcurrants
½ vanilla pod
3⅓ cups vodka, plus an extra ⅓–¾ cup
1 cup superfine granulated sugar for
   every 2 cups of liquid

makes
4 x 17-ounce or 2 x 1-liter bottles

how to drink
drizzle half a shot into a glass of champagne, cava, or prosecco to make a kir royale, or into white wine to make a kir

- Put the blackcurrants into a cooled, dry, sterilized, large, wide-rimmed 8-cup jar and muddle/mash with the end of a flat-ended, wooden rolling pin.
- Split the vanilla pod lengthwise, remove the seeds, then add both seeds and pod to the jar, cover with 3⅓ cups vodka, seal, and gently rock the jar.
- Leave to macerate for up to 2 months in a cool, dark place, gently rocking the mixture weekly.
- After this time, strain the infused alcohol through a fine-mesh sieve, discarding the pulp and vanilla pod.
- Measure the blackcurrant liquid and put it into a large, heavy-bottomed pan. For every 2 cups of sieved liquid, add in ¾ cup sugar and an extra ⅓ cup of vodka.
- Warm gently on a low heat, slowly stirring, dissolving the sugar without boiling, until it becomes a light syrup, about 15–20 minutes.
- Strain again through a muslin-lined fine-mesh sieve, pour into cooled, dry sterilized bottles, seal and leave to infuse for another 8 weeks before using.

Keeps for up to 1–2 years.

peach schnapps

If you have peaches lying around that are super-ripe, make them into peach schnapps. The bellini (a drizzle of peach schnapps topped with champagne) brings a sense of decadence to any dinner party and definitely deserves to come back in vogue.

12 ripe peaches
⅓ cup superfine granulated sugar
3 cups vodka

makes
4 x 17-ounce or 2 x 1-liter bottles

how to drink
in a bellini, served in a champagne flute or coupe with a Candied Kumquat (see page 214) on the side

- Remove the skins of the peaches by scoring the bottom with a cross, dipping them into boiling water for 1 minute, then into ice-cold water for another minute; the skins will peel off with ease. Roughly chop, keeping the stones.
- Put the peach flesh and stones into a cooled, dry, sterilized, large, wide-rimmed 8-cup jar and stir in the sugar. Cover with the vodka and seal.
- Leave to macerate in a dark place at room temperature for up to 2 months, gently rocking the mixture daily for 1 week to dissolve the sugar, then once a week thereafter.
- After this time, strain the infused vodka through a muslin-lined fine-mesh sieve and discard the stones and pulp.
- Return to your cleaned and sterilized jar and store/rest for another month.
- Strain again through a double muslin-lined fine-mesh sieve then pour into cooled, dry sterilized bottles and seal.

Keeps for up to 1–2 years.

spiced plum liqueur

This recipe is warm and invitingly cozy on cold nights. You can also use it in baking or marinating... it's versatile.

2 lbs red plums
1½ cups superfine granulated sugar
2 cups vodka
1 cup brandy
½ tsp ground cinnamon
½ tsp freshly grated or
   ground nutmeg

makes
4 x 17-ounce or 2 x 1-liter bottles

how to drink/eat
in a tumbler with ice. Or add to stewed fruit and use in a tart or pie

- Quarter the plums and discard the stones.
- Put the plums into a cooled, dry, sterilized, large, wide-rimmed 8-cup jar with the sugar and stir together.
- Add the vodka and brandy, seal the jar, and rock it gently.
- Leave to macerate in a dark place at room temperature for up to 2 months, gently shaking the mixture daily for 1 week to dissolve the sugar, then once a week thereafter.
- After this time, strain the infused vodka through a fine-mesh sieve, pressing it through with the back of a spoon, discarding any pulp.
- Re-strain through a muslin-lined fine-mesh sieve, to make the liqueur even clearer.
- Return to your cleaned and sterilized jar and store/rest for a further month.
- Strain a third time, using a double muslin-lined fine-mesh sieve, then pour into cooled, dry sterilized bottles and seal.

Keeps for up to 1–2 years.

limoncello

The first time I really enjoyed limoncello was in Puglia, Italy, sitting outside on a warm night, candles flickering and aromatic piles of olive tree leaves burning in the distance. It was homemade and tasted like Italian liquid gold.

12–14 lemons (very green, thick-skinned ones are best), peel only
4¼ cups vodka
4¼ cups water
4½ cups granulated sugar

makes
2 x 1-liter bottles

how to drink
keep in the freezer and serve ice-cold, as shots

- Peel the lemons with a vegetable peeler removing any white pith. Keep the peel and put the flesh aside to make something else (such as Lemonade, see page 238).
- Put the peel in a large, wide-rimmed 2.5–3 liter jar, cover with the vodka, seal tightly and leave to macerate for 10–20 days at room temperature. Don't move or be tempted to open the jar and keep it out of the sunlight.
- Put the water and sugar in a large, heavy bottomed pan and bring to boil, stirring to dissolve the sugar.
- Lower the heat and simmer for around 5–10 minutes. Remove from the heat and leave to cool for about an hour or keep in the fridge until ready to use.
- Add the cool syrup to the lemon-infused alcohol, seal and leave to macerate for another 10–20 days.
- After the second stage of maceration, strain the limoncello through a muslin-lined fine-mesh sieve, then pour the alcohol into cooled, dry sterilized bottles and seal. Keeps for up to 1–2 years.

meyer lemon-cello

Use the peel for this recipe and make marmalade from the flesh (see page 170).

6 Meyer lemons, peel only
2 cups vodka
2 cups water
2 cups granulated sugar

how to drink
pour from the freezer into shot glasses on hot summer nights as a digestif

- Peel the lemons with a vegetable peeler, removing as much white pith as you can. Follow the method steps for Limoncello above.

homemade triple sec

This bittersweet, orange-flavored liqueur from Curaçao, an island off the coast of Venezuela, is found in many of my favorite cocktails, like margaritas, Long Island ice teas, and cosmopolitans. I also like to just add hot water and sip it to warm the cockles on a cold winter's day.

3 tangerines
2–3 tangerines, juiced (you need ½ cup of juice)
2½ cups vodka
2 cups granulated sugar
1½ cups water
¼ tsp orange blossom water

makes
2 x 17-ounce or 1 1-liter bottle/s

how to drink
add to cocktails or, for a winter warmer, mix with hot water and serve with a cinnamon stick and a star anise float

- Slice the tangerines into ⅛-inch discs. Juice 2–3 tangerines until you get ½ cup of juice and put aside.
- Preheat the oven to the lowest possible setting, spread the tangerine discs evenly on a baking tray lined with baking parchment then bake them for 1–1½ hours until they are dehydrated but still sticky. Remove and cool to room temperature.
- Put the tangerine discs in a cooled, dry, sterilized, large, wide-rimmed 4-cup jar, cover with 1¼ cups of vodka, seal, and gently swirl the jar to mix everything up. Leave to infuse in a cool, dark place for 24–48 hours. Rock the jar intermittently.
- In another large, sterilized jar (as above), mix the remainder of the vodka with the tangerine juice, seal, swirl, and leave in the same place to infuse for the same amount of time.
- After this maceration period, strain both jars of infused spirits through a muslin-lined fine-mesh sieve, then strain again, this time using two pieces of muslin for a clearer liquid.
- Mix the sugar and water in a large, heavy-bottomed pan and gently bring to a low simmer for about 5 minutes, stirring until the sugar is completely dissolved and becomes a very light syrup. Remove and cool to room temperature.
- Combine the strained vodka with the sugar syrup and stir through the orange blossom water.
- Pour into cooled, dry, sterilized bottles, seal and store.

Keeps for up to 1–2 years.

mulled apple cider

It's autumn, a chill is in the air, and it's time to make a cup of mulled cider and watch the leaves float to the ground.

1 orange, zest and juice
3⅓ cups organic apple cider
3⅓ tbsp brandy
2 star anise
4 allspice berries
1 cinnamon stick
2 tbsp lemon juice
2 tbsp light or dark brown sugar,
  to taste

makes
about 4 cups

how to drink
served hot from a flask, while
outdoors or, if indoors, in mugs
by the fire

- Put everything into a medium, heavy-bottomed pan and very gently bring to a simmer, without boiling, for 10–15 minutes, stirring intermittently.
- Decant into a flask or ladle into individual mugs.

homemade bitters

Yes, cocktails again, this time concentrated tinctures. Just a drop or two of these will liven up any cocktail. In most cases, you use a non-flavored vodka to make up your bitter concoctions, but oak-aged flavors such as brandy or rye whiskey can also enhance your bitter. Once you have your basic tinctures straight, play around with different blends to create your new flavors.

makes
4 x 2 oz tincture bottles

how to drink
use to create your own cocktails
at home

A basic guide when making the initial straight bitters is to measure, by volume, 1 part dried botanicals to 5 parts spirits, or 1 part fresh botanicals to 2 parts spirits. Taste your blends as they macerate and adjust the levels of strength to your liking.

- For each recipe, put the herbs/spices/flavorings into a cooled, dry, sterilized jar (about 1 cup) that is big enough to hold all the dry and liquid ingredients. Pour the alcohol over, seal, and gently shake.
- Infuse in a cool, dark place for 2–20 days (depending on the herbs/spices/flavorings used, the tincture will take different times to macerate). Rock the jar and taste daily to check the strength. It will be intense, so dilute a drop or two in a little water to determine the true sense of the flavor. Add more herbs/spices/flavorings if you want a stronger tincture.
- When you decide it's ready, strain through a muslin-lined fine-mesh sieve, discard the pulp, repeat the straining with a clean piece of muslin for a clearer liquid, then pour into cooled, dry sterilized tincture bottles with dropper lids and seal.

These will keep for up to 6 months.

bitter blends to try

rose bitters

4 tsp edible dried rose petals
⅛ tsp vanilla seeds
¾ cup vodka

coffee bitters

25 coffee beans, muddled
1 tsp molasses
¼ cinnamon stick
¾ cup vodka

lavender bitters

4 tsp edible dried lavender
½ tsp honey
¼ orange, peel only (no pith)
¾ cup vodka

cardamom bitters

10 green cardamom pods, muddled
2 juniper berries
¾ cup vodka

angostura bitters

½ orange, peel only (no pith)
1 tbsp orange juice
½ cinnamon stick
1 tsp dried sour cherries
1 juniper berry
¼ tsp cassia chips
1 coffee bean
4 whole cloves
⅛ tsp wild cherry bark
⅛ tsp orris root
¼ vanilla pod, seeds only
½ tsp honey
¼ star anise
¾ cup rye whiskey

orange bitters

½ tsp honey
1 orange, peel only (pith removed)
4 whole cloves, muddled
2 green cardamom pods, muddled
¾ cup vodka

Angostura
Bitters
Coffee
Bitters

acknowledgments

This book has definitely been a collaboration. It's been a fun and sometimes full of emotion process but it would never have seen its rewarding completion without the following people who helped it along its journey. With many thanks.

Firstly to my husband, Mark, who not only beautifully designed this book, but supported me every step of the way as a very tolerant soundboard. And who is always there for me.

To my mother, for introducing me to various types of food while growing up, and my father, for all the great seafood.

To Karolina Stein, assistant, friend, and such a hard, hard worker, you're the boss. And to my staff along the way, Sarah, Beni, Tess, and my mother-in-law Kate.

To Rowan Yapp (for making such delicious thumbprint cookies), Dan Crissman, and the teams at Penguin Random House in the UK and Norton in the US, thank you for putting up with all of my many queries and believing in this book from the word go.

To Philippa Langley at foxandfavour.co.uk. Your energy and photography are inspiring—I can't wait to work with you again.

To Rob Shreeve, for all your invaluable advice as my literary agent.

Thank you Kate Ruth, for your personal styling help—you are a star.

Sara Dunlop, Melissa, and Charlie at jamjarflowers.co.uk and Anna Hart for lending me their beautiful homes to shoot in.

Dr. Benedict Smith for your award-winning chili jam recipe.
A.D. Schierning for your homemade tomato ketchup inspiration.
To Bao London for the Bao buns for my plum sauce—baolondon.com

Kevin, Eddy, and Chris at the New Spitalfields market, thank you for putting up with my sleepy eyes and yawns at 6am in the morning.
To all my delis, shops, cafés, pubs, and regular customers who have been supporting Newton & Pott and the growth of local business in the community.

And finally to those who kindly lent their beautifully crafted wares for the images in this book:
Meighan Ellis with Relic.Ceramics—meighan@meighanellis.com
Jane Sarre Ceramics—janesarre.co.uk
Jonty Hampson—hampsonwoods.com
And Joi for her beautiful Irish linens—31chapellane.com

index

about kylee newton

Kylee Newton is a New Zealander who has lived in East London for the past 15 years. She is a passionate self-taught preserver who began making chutneys seven years ago as homemade gifts for friends. She now runs a successful preserves business called Newton & Pott. As well as making preserves each week for her stall at Broadway Market, she also sells her goods to various delis, pantries, and cafés across London. Something she loves about preserving is the blend of the new and the old: both testing new flavor combinations and rediscovering age-old methods. She does collaborations with like-minded food producers.